Piecing Your Heart Back Together

Advance Praise

"The exercises she walks you through are outstanding! I truly felt like I got to know myself more in the process."
— **Tammy Hall**, Life Coach and Teacher

PIECING YOUR HEART BACK TOGETHER

The Road Map *to* Healing *and* Thriving *after a* Breakup *or* Divorce

CARMEN SILVESTRO

NEW YORK

LONDON • NASHVILLE • MELBOURNE • VANCOUVER

PIECING YOUR HEART BACK TOGETHER

The Road Map to Healing and Thriving After a Breakup or Divorce

Published in New York, New York, by Morgan James Publishing in partnership with Difference Press. Morgan James is a trademark of Morgan James, LLC. www.MorganJamesPublishing.com

ISBN 9781631950933 paperback
ISBN 9781631950940 eBook
ISBN 9781631950957 audio
Library of Congress Control Number: 2020934384

Cover Design Concept: Jennifer Stimson

Cover Design: Christopher Kirk www.GFSstudio.com

Interior Design: Chris Treccani www.3dogcreative.net

Editor: Nkechi Obi

Book Coaching: The Author Incubator

Author Photo: Ari Scott Photography

Morgan James is a proud partner of Habitat for Humanity Peninsula and Greater Williamsburg. Partners in building since 2006.

Get involved today! Visit
MorganJamesPublishing.com/giving-back

For Carter, my sunshine and my beautiful spirited son.
Thank you for inspiring me every single day.
May you never stop pursuing the life of your dreams.
I love you with all my heart!

— Mom

Table of Contents

Foreword   xi

Introduction   xv

Chapter 1:   My Story—Endings Are Beginnings   1

Chapter 2:   The Healing Process   9

Chapter 3:   Soothing the Loss   15

Chapter 4:   Intentions—Compass for Life   41

Chapter 5:   Acceptance   51

Chapter 6:   Self-Awareness—Time Alone
              a New Best Friend   67

Chapter 7:   I Forgive You and I Release You   83

Chapter 8:   Rewrite Your Story and Change
              the Paradigm   93

Chapter 9:   Become Inspired and Inspire Others   103

Chapter 10:   Obstacles   107

Chapter 11:   Conclusion   111

Acknowledgments   117
Thank You   119
About the Author   121

Foreword

Don't you worry, dear one. No matter how much you're hurting right now, if you are reading this book, you are held in love.

When I met Carmen Silvestro, I saw this beautiful, bubbly, caring woman. Once I read her book, I knew we were sister-warriors from another life. Or, simply, two women who experienced the same journey called "divorce" and came out of it victorious.

Carmen's book plunged me a few years back into the past. Her journey is so similar to mine, and it feels so similar to the stories I've heard over the years from so many of my own clients. It's a story of experiencing pain beyond anything imaginable, of letting go of everything you thought was true, of forgiving those who hurt you the most, and of allowing yourself to listen to your own wisdom in a way you may never have experienced before. And finally, this is a story of stepping out on the other side of this dark path, so you can feel strong, powerful, and know that even though it was not easy, this divorce might actually be one of the best things that ever happened to you.

Divorce and breakup happen to so many of us and, still, if you want to come out of it feeling a sense of hope and even excitement, you might want to get some support from someone, like Carmen, who really understands this process. Reading *Piecing Your Heart Back Together* may actually be your first step in going from wondering, "Why is this happening to me?" to asking, "How can I grow from this journey?"

What makes this book so powerful is that it's a genuine, authentic download from Carmen's heart directly to yours. Over the pages, she shares the story of her own pain but, more importantly, she shares essential and simple tools in small digestible bites to help anybody going through heartbreak fully let go and reinvent themselves. Whether she talks about finding your own emotional freedom, acceptance, or forgiveness, her message is one of hope, wisdom and inspiration, and you will find the words comforting for wherever you are in your own process.

Your heart might feel tender right now, but don't delay! It's essential to know that there are steps you can take to not only heal your wounds, but also rediscover this amazing person you are. Open the book at the first page and start *Healing and Thriving after your Breakup or Divorce*. You're not alone. In Carmen Silvestro, you will find a companion, a best friend, a guide to hold your hand in your darkest moments, and you will emerge free, peaceful, and strong.

With Love,
Dr. Fabienne, "Fab," Slama
www.fabyoulicious.com

Introduction

ello, my dearest one. I know how devastating this is. No matter the circumstances, when you lose someone you love, you are grieving. No one understands the kind of pain you are going through unless they have gone through it themselves. The sleepless nights, the endless tears, and the feeling of frailty. Feeling like you can't breathe when you try to imagine your life without your partner, your best friend. Your world is falling apart piece by piece, and you no longer have your ex to hold your hand through it. It's as if you have been tossed into an abyss with no sign of a familiar road, light, or hope anywhere in sight. Sometimes you feel like you are in a devastatingly bad dream that you can't wake yourself from, where not even the salty tears that run from the sides of your eyelids or the quivering sounds from your mouth can wake you. It is like a nightmare for sure. Except it's real.

When your phone rings, you secretly hope it's going to be your ex, begging for forgiveness and acknowledging the huge mistake you are both making. "Let's not give up! I love you," he will desperately say. But it never happens. Instead, he grows colder and more distant by the day. His indifferent eyes look at you as if you never meant anything to him.

Work is getting very tricky to say the least. There are days when you are successful. On these days, you manage to throw yourself head first into tasks where you fully, and purposefully, immerse yourself and obsess over every detail, knowing full well that if you break your concentration or let your mind wander off, *he* will creep back in. You may find yourself revisiting old memories of the two of you and wondering how you got to this place. You will find yourself holding back a thousand tears and wondering if you will ever feel happiness again. Will that ever be possible?

Loved ones are so supportive. They try their best to keep you strong and cheer you up, but even a smile causes you physical pain. You are feeling how unbearable you have become and can hardly stand to look at yourself in the mirror, so you start to retreat into solitude. You have your family and friends, yet you have never felt so alone.

There are days when you just want to pull the covers over your head and block out the world. You want to stay where you are and not have to talk or answer when someone asks how you are feeling today with that look of pity. And there are days when you want to curl up with your anger and pain, where you feel justified to stay in this dark place and never come out again. You feel frozen and unable to let go of the suffering.

Sometimes, in the middle of showering, you realize you have drifted off again into the middle of a memory when things were so easy and free and full of love, when you used to stay up all night talking and laughing or make love until the sun came up. It's a memory that starts off sweetly but, moments later, sends you into a sobbing frenzy where you have to hold on to the shower walls for strength. You almost wish you could go back in time and prevent ever meeting him. I know.

I also know that what you want now more than anything is to heal and get past this torment that seems to be ruining your life. I know you dream of the days when you can finally stop wasting your time with obsessive thoughts about your ex, to the days when you no longer allow your mind to wander off or derail you (day and night) with torturous feelings. You want to move on and not feel this haunting pain any longer. You want to be able to eat a meal again and enjoy it. You want to be able to sleep through the night and feel rested the next morning. You want to be present for your loved ones and be able to concentrate and be your best at work again. You would do anything to make this pain go away and get your life back. You would do anything to be able to feel a real smile or laughter come over you again. I know.

Don't give up, my dear one. I promise, where you are is only temporary.

Chapter 1:

My Story—Endings Are Beginnings

When I found out my ex-husband was having an affair, there was the obvious shock and anger—anger over the betrayal that he was not who I thought he was. The man I married would not pursue another woman. He was above this. People who have affairs are weak and immoral. This was not my husband. My husband had integrity. He was loving and honest. For years, he had pursued me and told me how he wished for me. He wrote me songs and left me little love notes on the bathroom mirror after he took a hot shower. He was my best friend in the world. I knew everything about him, and he knew everything about me. We had been through wars and glory days together. We were even trying to have a child! So, it was just not possible that this was the same man. For a few hours after I found out he was involved with someone else, I was livid. I thought I was better off without him. If *he* would do this to me, and *she* would get involved with a married man, then they deserved one another, and I was done. This was what I felt for about five hours.

It was a Saturday night. My husband left for the night to play with his band at the Borgata in Atlantic City. I had decided to stay home this time because I was tired from doing a lot of work on our new home. I was also emotionally drained. I really didn't want to sit through a night of loud music, too many drunk guys, and me having a drink too many. Not tonight. Tonight, I would do my best to leave sadness and worry behind. I would relax and do something for myself.

My little brother would have wanted me to. He had passed away a month prior, and for a month, I had turned into my mom. I carried a planet of pain and worry for my family on my shoulders. So tonight was going to be different. It would be about celebrating my decorating skills and relaxing with some music, pictures, and a glass of wine.

"Pier 1 never saw me coming," I chuckled. We were up to our elbows in decorative pillows, bamboo plants, healing rocks, and all kinds of wall hangings. This was my therapy. My husband knew how much I loved and supported him, so skipping a show once in a while was no biggie. I had always encouraged him to play music and to follow his dreams, and I always listened to him talk music 24/7.

Yes, things had become a little mundane and gloomy lately, to say the least, with my little brother's passing. We had our problems here and there, but what marriage didn't have problems? There was nothing I saw as earth shattering.

My job had become nothing but a paycheck. At the time, I was the accounting and human resources manager at my company and was coming up on twenty years, but for the past year, the terrible stress and long hours since the new owner took over, had taken their toll on me. But still I felt stuck there since we were now "proud" owners of a home. Eric was unhappy about his day job too. He was the purchasing manager for a music company, and his career had reached its peak a while back. It was not satisfying anymore, so he was starting to scout other companies. Even his beloved band had broken up, and his new band was not what he hoped it would be. He was no longer the center of attention. This band had a lead guitarist already. For my husband, who was pretty amazing and admired as a guitar player, that was really a major step back. There was a different vibe at his shows and with his playing. I could sense a totally different energy coming from him on that stage. He didn't look happy, but the look in his eyes was more than just unhappiness in his new role—he seemed pretty tired. Still, we loved each other and would always find ways to lift each other up. That's what we did.

It was pretty late at night. I was sitting at home looking through some old pictures on our home computer. I came across pictures from our honeymoon in the Bahamas. We really had a great time there and swore we would go back someday. On the last day of our trip, we were supposed to go scuba diving but ended up on the beach drinking piña coladas all day instead. *Maybe this year we could revisit and go on that excursion*, I thought. Our wedding anniversary was coming up, so this would be ideal. As always, there were a few blurry shots I had to delete along the way. After a few too many like this, I decided to just quickly sift through the rest of the pictures when something caught my eye. It was an unnamed document, and to this day, I am not sure what made me click into it. Some might say that this was intuition at its finest.

I can still remember the gut-wrenching feeling in my stomach as I read the contents of this email. It was a love letter from my husband to another woman. He was contemplating leaving me. I saw a white light come over me, like an out-of-body experience. As I read the email, I went cold. My veins felt as cold as ice.

No! This is not happening.

I grabbed a pillow and screamed into it. But no sound came out as I screamed. My body was too shocked to let any sound come out. And there, plain as day, was the opened document on my desktop. I read it again, and then one more time, before I jumped out of my chair and began to pace the room. *What do I do? Do I call anyone? Yes, I have to. I am going to go crazy. What if this is a mistake? How embarrassing it would be if it were a misunderstanding. Do I leave? Do I kick him out? Do I wait for him to get home and confront him? What on earth do I do? Please, God. Please help me. I beg you to give me strength. I don't want my marriage to be over. Tell me what to do!*

I grabbed the phone and called my sister, Jackie, who lived only a few blocks away. She picked up the phone, clearly half asleep, and I screamed into the phone. I could hardly make any sense, but my sister knew me well enough to know I was in big trouble. I tried to calm myself and began to tell her about the letter. *"Eric is either having an affair or is about to have one,"* I said. After reading her the whole message, I sobbed uncontrollably. I think I sobbed daily for a month from that day forward.

Eric and I met at a Halloween party. We were both eighteen years old. He was a sweet, loving guy with the biggest smile. At the time, I had more of an aloof, hard exterior, so I found him adorable, but not dating material. Having been through a few rough times in my life, I was not really sure of who I was or what I wanted. But I definitely knew I was not emotionally available to be in a serious relationship, especially with someone so genuine and kind. Still, he persisted.

He called, and he waited. He called and waited some more. Finding his persistence so sweet, I started to really trust him and confide in him. We developed a great friendship. Soon, we had turned into best friends. A couple of years later, we were a couple, and then we got married. We were a completely unstoppable couple and were head over heels for one another. It was true love. It was what poets wrote about in their journals.

His family was not crazy about me at first, and this certainly caused friction in our relationship; still, we persevered. This was not the type of love you found at a bar. For me, it was like I had found my knight in shining armor.

When I handed my husband the suitcases and kindly told him to go ahead and take some time away, I was convinced I was doing the right thing. He seemed lost and full of pain, so I wanted him to take a breather. I was worried about him regardless of what he had done. I also thought it would be good for both of us to take some time apart. I was still trying to wrap my head around what had occurred and was also blaming myself completely for his infidelity. But I really never thought he would go through with the other woman. I still thought he was a decent man who just needed to get his head together. We had spent seventeen years of our lives together, so I thought he would keep that in mind and not throw away our marriage so easily.

I was wrong. It seems I was wrong about many things regarding my relationship and my marriage. My husband and I were going through a divorce.

My little brother had passed away, and my marriage was suddenly dead. My world was collapsing, and it became too much for me to handle on my own, so I started seeking therapy.

My divorce was not easy by any means. Accepting that my marriage was over was extremely difficult. The heartbreak from this loss was the most excruciating and painful experience I have ever been though. The first couple of weeks were the darkest I have ever felt. But I never gave up.

I remember one day, I was on my kitchen floor, surrounded by a sea of Kleenex, feeling completely empty. I had literally run out of tears. My eyes felt thick and puffy. I decided to look at myself in the bathroom mirror, and I gasped at the face looking back at me. I looked like a punching bag. My body looked so frail from losing twenty pounds. For an already thin person, this was a lot. This was the day I decided I had enough. I was not going to drop anchor here.

Through my determination, self-help books, therapy, and my amazing support system of family and friends, I was able to get stronger and move through the grief, blame, and judgment. I learned so much along the journey. One of the most valuable lessons that I learned was that a broken heart is also an open heart. When your heart has been opened, it is exposing all the parts of you that have been left unhealed, and it brings to the surface all of the unresolved issues from your past. I also came to realize that my marriage was my hide out. The reason why I held on to my marriage so tightly was not so much about my ex at all but about me wanting to be hidden. My feelings of desperation were about me trying to escape whoever I really was. It was about containing my self-loathing and wanting to stand behind someone who was admired and loved. I was looking to feel normal and loved.

Once I was able to figure out the areas in my life I needed to work on, I realized that I had to go back and dive deep to uncover layers of myself. That's when things clicked. I was putting together a puzzle, piece by piece, and discovering the very essence of who I was; the strong, determined, and valuable being that I am. Although it was frustrating at times, and it took a little while to feel healthy and confident again, the journey, experiences, and aha moments I experienced along the way were priceless!

There really is a silver lining to your heartbreak. When I changed the way I viewed the loss of my marriage, I realized that endings are really new beginnings and the devastating pain, if you work through it, can bring you to a whole new place of love, gratitude, peace, and joy—a place where you can release old pain that has been stored inside of you and a place where you are motivated to start over with new perspective, purpose, curiosity, and tools to navigate life in a whole different way. With a little help, openness, and willingness, you can use this breakup as the time to change your life forever and for the better!

> *"Remember that not getting what you want is*
> *sometimes a wonderful stroke of luck."*
> — Dalai Lama

Chapter 2:

The Healing Process

When I went through my divorce, I was so haunted by the pain that I experienced that I committed to helping others get through their breakup and divorce. Through trial and error, and with a little help from my therapist, self-help books, personal hurdles, and what I have learned through coaching clients, I have been able to put together this book as a life-changing way to get you through to the other side with a whole new outlook of yourself and your life. You don't need to wait years to recover from your broken heart; you can begin your healing path today.

My hope is that you use this book as a roadmap, to get you from where you are right now to a life that you never thought was possible. Make a commitment, do the work, and follow this method so you can begin healing and transforming your life!

To be successful at getting over your breakup, you must observe, acknowledge, and work through your feelings. You must be able to look at the relationship in a new light, accept the outcome, and forgive. Charles R. Swindoll says, "life is 10 percent what happens to you and 90 percent how you react to it." That's why I created my healing process to offer you the chance to react in the most valuable way, to believe in yourself, and rewrite your story.

Through my healing process, we will be diving into seven steps. You will also notice that at the beginning of each chapter, I mention a few crystals. Although it's not necessary to use these, crystals have been around since ancient times as a form of medicine. They are each filled with their own healing properties for the mind, body, and soul and are said to promote good energy and get rid of negative energy. So, if you are open-minded, why not give them a try?

Soothing the Loss

In this chapter, I am going to walk you through powerful techniques you can start using today that will help you move through your emotions, release negative energy, and erase limiting beliefs so that you don't seek to numb or run away from your painful emotions. I will explain why cutting all contact with your ex is a must and how journaling your relationship from a different lens is important, and you will also learn meditations and other key exercises that will change how you see your breakup.

Intention

This is probably the most important step in this book because setting intentions will not only help you stay on course, focused, and committed to your healing process, but it will be the foundation to your recovery goals and what keeps you motivated and moving forward. In this chapter, you will also learn about affirmations and gratitude and their immense role in your recovery.

Acceptance

In this chapter we will discuss how resistance to the present can actually cause you greater pain and suffering and how if you are not careful, you can get stuck in denial or avoidance behaviors that will keep you from ever moving forward in life. You will learn how choosing acceptance will actually help you release the attachment and go through the process of healing much faster. We will also talk about practicing self-love and self-compassion, and we will discuss the biggest mistakes people make when grieving the end of a relationship.

Self-Awareness

You will finally have a chance to get to know yourself in a completely different way and you will see how this time alone is actually an amazing gift. In this chapter, you will learn to reclaim yourself, and think outside the box with some great exercises that I put together that will help you get really clear about what you want. You will learn techniques to dive into the heart of your being and become excited about your future.

I Forgive You and I Release You

In this chapter, you will learn about self-forgiveness and forgiving your ex-partner (even when there is no apology). We will talk about the most important letter that you will write. You will learn techniques and rituals to assist you in the process of forgiving and letting go of negative emotions that no longer serve you.

Rewrite Your Story

Now that you are in a new chapter of your life, this is the time to add new practices to help you manifest your deepest desires. In this step, you will learn about how visualization can put you in the space for receiving what you want, how taking self-inventory will help you realize and remove old habits or enculturation that are holding you back, and how tapping into your spirituality, or getting curious about it now, will help transform you and align you with your truest self, as well as other acts that you can do to open yourself up to a new amazing life.

Become Inspired/Be an Inspiration

In this last step, you will learn about sharing your enthusiasm and becoming an inspiration and hope for others who are struggling. You will not only learn how paying it forward affects others, but also how it impacts you on your new journey. We will discuss the several obstacles that show up to try to keep you from healing and changing and how this breakup can actually be the best thing that has ever happened to you.

I know how you feel, and there is nothing more that I want than to hear about how you conquered this heartbreak and have become the deliberate creator of your life. I am honored to be here for you every step of the way on your beautiful unique healing path.

Chapter 3:

Soothing the Loss

Healing Crystals: Kunzite, Amethyst, Brown Goldstone

Going through a divorce or a breakup, especially after it's been years of being together, is excruciatingly painful. You are grieving and your body and mind are going through a mob of different emotions all day long. Your brain doesn't just fall out of love, so you are filled with this intense pain, this void, and feelings of abandonment and rejection because you no longer have access to your ex. But I promise that if you hang in there with me, and do the work, you will get through this. The most important thing right now is that you don't try to escape it. We are going to work through all of this in a very healthy way.

While it is very important not to run away from your emotions, it is just as important not to stay with this negative energy inside of you. As I am sure you already know, this can impact your life in a massive way. In time, it can endanger your health. We all know that stress is a silent killer, so the last thing we want to do is put your well-being in jeopardy. So instead of keeping your emotions bottled up inside and in order for you to truly heal, let's start to work through these emotions and release them.

In this book, I am going to talk to you about a few techniques that helped me do just that. The more you put these into practice, the more you will notice major improvements and feelings of peace. Eventually, your negative feelings about your divorce or breakup will be gone. You will notice that you can retell the story to someone but not feel immersed in the pain of it. The horrible, painful emotions that were once attached to your story will no longer be present. It is really remarkable. So, let's take this one day at a time and one piece at a time, okay?

Emotional Freedom Technique

When I first heard about this technique, it wasn't mainstream talk or anything that I had heard of before, so when my therapist introduced me to it, I admit I was a bit skeptical. However, I had been doing so much self-development and put in so much work into my healing that I was open to try anything.

She initially brought this technique up when I complained that, although I was in a much better place emotionally, I was still unable to hold back the tears whenever I told my story to anyone. It turned out that even though I was in a much better place, I had a lot of negative energy stored inside of my body that I needed to release. Once I began using this technique, even from the first session, I instantly felt so much lighter! For me, it was a miraculous experience.

Emotional freedom technique (EFT), or "tapping," is an alternative treatment for emotional distress. It is used for trauma, fears, and anxiety. EFT involves tapping near the end points of "energy meridians" (acupuncture points) located around the body. Basically, it is tapping your energy points and releasing the crud while saying mantras. It is believed that this type of tapping of the body can create a balance in your energy system and treat emotional and physical pain. Sounds kind of weird? Don't worry, when you open your mind and begin this technique, you will feel the release, and it won't be weird anymore.

EFT is meant to help release the negative energy brought out by your emotions and help you to accept yourself regardless of what you are feeling right now. It will help you cope with the feelings of abandonment or rejection, and oftentimes, it helps release other old emotions that are stuck inside of you and helps you let go of self-limiting beliefs that are keeping you stuck and preventing you from moving forward.

Remember, although it is normal for people to beat themselves up or get down on themselves after a failed marriage or relationship, it is not okay to stay in this place. This technique will help you accept the situation the way it is and accept yourself and your reaction to what is happening. It will help you to feel at peace with yourself.

EFT Exercise

This exercise will essentially allow you to embrace your emotions, so that you can work through them, and eventually let them go. Take note of the emotion that you are feeling right now and write down on a scale of one to ten how intense this emotion is.

There are two steps to this technique: one is the physical (tapping) and the other one is verbal (mantras). Below are a few examples of the verbal statements that you can say while tapping on your points to help accept and release the negative about your breakup. Fill in whatever emotion you are going through right now.

Here are some examples of mantras that you can say:

- Even though I feel hurt, rejected, and abandoned by my ex, I love and accept myself deeply and completely.
- Even though I am shocked, angry, and devastated that my ex had an affair, I love and accept myself deeply and completely.

- Even though I feel hatred toward my ex, I can't believe he threw our marriage away. I love and accept myself deeply and completely.
- Even though I feel (you fill in the blank), I love and accept myself deeply and completely.

There are so many statements you can make up. Once you become more familiar with this process, you will have no problem writing one that resonates with you, but for now, start with these, edit them as you need to, and use any others that come up for you when you become in tune with your feelings.

You will follow your mantras with another round; only this time, you will be saying positive mantras:

- I am open to the possibility that I can begin to let go
- I am open to softening these intense feelings
- It's okay to let this go and begin to heal
- I am open to the possibility of feeling happiness again
- I am open to the possibility of letting go of this sadness and seeing the light that surrounds me
- I am open to choosing peace and love and finding softer feelings
- I am so grateful for the support I have all around me
- I believe in myself and my ability to create healing and happiness again.

How do you feel? Rate on a scale of one to ten the strength of your emotion. By the end of this exercise, you should feel calmer, but if you don't, repeat the technique until the strength of your emotion drops down to around a three or less.

Use this link to watch my EFT video demonstration:
https://www.youtube.com/watch?
v=UqWzwjGPCgg&feature=youtu.be

One of the things I find really amazing is that oftentimes while doing this process for myself or with my clients, old stuff comes up we didn't even realize was there! It is truly cathartic. For example, while tapping to release some of his anger toward his ex, one of my clients recalled a childhood memory of when his father made him feel like he was worthless. Although he and his father were in a good place and had already worked through their issues years earlier, there was negative energy still attached inside his body. Once this came up and he "tapped" it out, he felt an immense sense of relief.

Remember, you cannot run away from your emotions. Many people try to suppress their emotions or try to cover them up with a new relationship, work, or drugs and alcohol. They may think they need to be strong and pretend everything is just fine. But what they don't realize is that they need to go through their emotions in order to heal. Otherwise, these will just manifest themselves in other relationships or parts of their lives in very negative ways.

Using EFT, and the other techniques that I will go over with you, will help you cope and release the negative. Whatever feelings or emotions come up, give yourself full permission to let them be. You will find inner peace and healing.

Below is a diagram of the tapping points for EFT. Before you begin, close your eyes for a second and feel your emotion. Rate yourself on a scale of one to ten on how strong this emotion feels, and do the tapping exercise until you are down to a two or three.

Emotional Freedom Technique—EFT Tapping Points

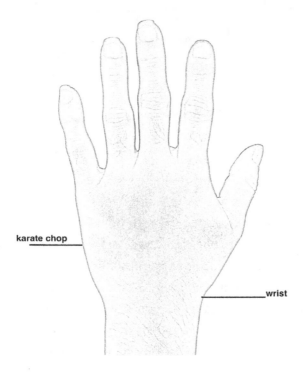

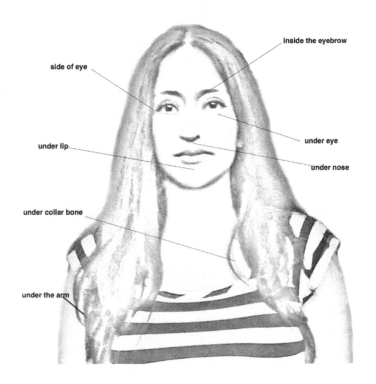

side of eye

inside the eyebrow

under eye

under lip

under nose

under collar bone

under the arm

Relationship Rehab

No Contact Agreement

I remember long ago hearing someone say that they wished their ex was dead. And I remember being shocked and thinking that this was such a horrible thing to wish or say about anyone. However, as I was judging, I had no idea the amount of pain and suffering this person was going through at the time. Years later, I found out that what she really meant was that it would be easier for her to get through the pain and loss if her ex was not around, especially since he had already moved on with someone else. The anxiety of possibly running into them was like an extra dagger in her heart that kept her paralyzed and incapable of moving forward for many years. And knowing that he was so close kept her obsessed with his life and his whereabouts. She admitted to driving by his house and work and calling his phone and hanging up constantly. This is why it is so important that you make the commitment to completely break all contact with your ex. The sooner you can disconnect, the faster you can begin healing. Because of this incident, and so many more similar stories, I became inspired to come up with the next crucial step in your recovery: the "No Contact Agreement."

Many studies have found that the feeling of rejection stemming from a breakup sends signals to your brain that initiate chemical reactions in your body similar to those experienced during drug withdrawal, creating this painful void that you are desperately trying to fill. According to research from Stony Brook University, "Love is comparable to drug addiction. It activates parts of the brain associated with motivation and reward." This explains why, when we no longer have access to our partner, we feel the excruciating pain of abandonment and an intense craving for our partner (our drug).

When my marriage was ending, the thought of not speaking to my partner everyday was unimaginable. We had been in each other's lives for seventeen years. How was I supposed to just cut off all ties with him? I remember one day I drove to his job and had him come outside to talk to me. I could feel his coworkers looking at us through the office windows, but I didn't care. I really didn't know what I was even going to say; I just needed to be around him. I just couldn't let go. It was extremely difficult for me to walk away, especially in the beginning. I felt like I physically needed to be around him because everything in my body hurt. It was much worse than when I quit smoking. It was like the worst addiction ever.

It is important for you to understand the importance of completely cutting off contact with your ex. You have to break the addiction. Once you cut ties with them, you will start to feel better. You will be able to breathe and start moving forward.

One of the biggest reasons many of my clients struggle so much through their breakups or keep having setbacks is because they will not stop communicating with their exes. There are so many reasons (excuses) you will tell yourself to stay in touch. We will talk about that in a minute, but you need to understand that all this is doing is literally prolonging your suffering. In order to truly get past your breakup or divorce, you have to separate yourself both physically and emotionally from your ex.

In this day and age, with so many different ways of communicating, you have to make it a conscious decision to cut off contact with your ex. It is crucial that you make the commitment to stop calling, emailing, posting on their social media, and doing drive-bys at their house or wherever they hang out. It is just as important not to be available to see them or answer if they try to contact you. It is understandable how an innocent "like" on their Facebook picture or a quick "hello" text can seem harmless enough, right? I mean you have shared a life together, so this seems small enough. But trust me, you are only fooling yourself. You have to ask yourself what the end game is. Be really honest about what you are really trying to accomplish and, most importantly, what it will cost you when you don't get the result that you were really seeking. There is nothing light about having to deal with the additional suffering this will bring you. You have to let go, or you will find yourself trapped in the hamster wheel.

Letting go is extremely challenging. There will be moments when it is harder than others. There will be days, like holidays or special trips or when you hear a song that was memorable to the two of you, where you miss them the most and you are so tempted to reach out. These are the times when you especially have to resist and remind yourself that you cannot go down that road! I can't express enough how important it is that you don't! Don't give in. This moment will pass.

I remember the first time, after being officially divorced, I heard my wedding song play on the radio. It was "From This Moment On" by Shania Twain. My stomach turned into a giant knot, and I felt cold and faint—I couldn't breathe. Well, guess what? It passed. It will pass for you, too, and you will feel so great once you keep letting these moments pass and you don't react to them. I know, you might be thinking that your situation is different, that there really are reasons for you to keep an open door. Unless you have children, which I will talk about later, there is no reason to stay in touch. Think about your sanity.

Here are some of the most common excuses from and my responses to my clients who tried to stay in touch with their exes:

Excuse	Response
I just want to be friends.	You cannot be friends or friends with benefits.
I want closure.	Give yourself closure.
What if they want to reconcile?	Finish reading this book.
They left some things behind.	Ditch the stuff. You don't need to give it back.
We share friends, and they hang out at the same places.	This can get a little tricky, but this always gets resolved among them. The important thing is that you discuss with your friends the importance of your recovery and why you cannot go to the places you went with them for now. Your friends will understand. Once you get past this phase, you will actually want to go to these places and make new memories.
I feel lonely or am having a problem and want to talk to someone who really knows me.	Call another friend or family member, or go to your support group.

I know how painful it is to go through your days without your partner. In the beginning, days without them will be the longest, and sitting with this hurt can easily make you feel like you are too weak to resist contacting them. Remember, it's the same as quitting an addiction. But the fact that you are reading this book tells me you are ready to do what it takes to break yourself free from this addiction and from this suffering. So, hang in there. No one said it's going to be easy, but you should commit because the reward will be like no other. You will feel this pass, and see your new life ahead, and trust me it looks amazing!

Okay, time to roll up your sleeves.

The No Contact Contract

The first thing you need to do is set the intention to cut off all contact with your ex and make a contract with yourself. This means deleting old texts, pictures, emails, and messages. You need to make a conscious decision not to go onto their social media. Blocking them would be a great idea. Make a commitment to stop going to restaurants or bars that you know your ex goes to with hopes of "accidentally" running into them. Make a promise to not call or text them, and do not post messages about where you are going, hoping that they show up there. Yes, I have heard all the tricks! Get a piece of paper and make the agreement now.

I, _____, on the date of _____ do hereby declare my intention: I give my personal promise not to call, text, instant message, email, or mail my ex. Furthermore, I am unfriending, unfollowing, and blocking him/her from my social media. I refrain from going to spots where I know he/she frequents, and I will not check his/her social media, or any other medium, to have access to him/her. My goal is to emotionally detach myself from my ex. I am empowered and taking back control of my life. I am healing and embracing my amazing new life journey.

_____   _____
Signature   Date

Keep this agreement always handy. Tape it to your mirror; make copies and put it around your house if you need to; and keep it in your wallet.

If You Have Children Together

You can absolutely keep the No Contact Contract Agreement even if you have kids together. Communicate by email only. Keep only the emergency number that you need. Use a court-appointed email system if you need to, but make sure to respond with yes or no answers only. Do not engage in any discussions or arguments. Stick to yes or no.

Do not go to events you know your ex is attending. This is very important, at least until you are emotionally ready and much further into the healing process.

Essentially you want to remove any and all contact with your ex. Make sure you set some guidelines and boundaries for an emergency. Do not let them break these boundaries, and you, yourself, do not break your own boundaries!

My client was completely baffled when he got dumped. As far as he knew, things were moving along great. They were together for almost two years, and he was contemplating popping the big question in the next few months when out of nowhere he got the boot. To make matters worse, she hardly had much to say about the reasons behind the breakup. He came to find out that she had found someone else and had already started seeing him a month before she dumped him. He became obsessed and started self-blaming. He kept calling and texting her, trying to convince her to give him another chance. He followed her on her social media daily, and he kept reading the texts and emails that they shared in the past.

My client didn't realize that because he wasn't taking a breather and disconnecting from her, he wasn't taking the opportunity to step back and look at the relationship from a different perspective. He was looking and speaking about her like she was this perfect goddess. Once he made the commitment to cut ties, remove old emails, and stop following her, he was able to see his ex in a whole new light. He realized that she was actually pretty manipulative and dishonest and that all along, she was mostly just using him to pay her bills. Needless to say, my client was disgusted and angry. He was able to shut that door and lock it.

Gathering Your Angel Team

Now it's time to make a list of a group of people, such as family and friends, who will support you in your healing and will be there when you feel like temptation is great. Make sure that someone is a person you can call immediately when you are having one of those rough days at work, or when you feel lonely and sad or feel like you are especially vulnerable. Make a list now of friends, relatives, support groups, or places of worship. Make them aware of your situation. There are now both online and face-to-face support groups. Reach out to them. Keep strong. You got this!

Dethroning Them

When a relationship ends, especially when it was not by our choice, we tend to go into desperation mode. Part of that can mean over idealizing your ex and thinking of your relationship as some perfect masterpiece that was your only chance at love and happiness. You tend to get a warped sense of reality when you look at your relationship and think about your ex. You tend to romanticize your entire relationship and think of every single little good thing that happened and enlarge it in your mind by 100 percent. You only remember how good things were in the beginning and your memories of bliss.

The reason you do that has to do with your brain being stuck in reconciling mode. It wants so desperately to fill that void—that feeling of abandonment—and get the thing back that you no longer have—your ex. You are so clouded by the agonizing feelings of rejection that you lose sense of what's real.

The problem is that until I can get you to look at your ex and your relationship as a whole, with a clearer perspective, you run the risk of getting stuck on the hamster wheel. You could end up spending months or maybe years pining for them without moving forward. As the Law of Attraction says, your thoughts are like a magnet. You get what you put out there. We will talk more about the Law of Attraction in later chapters. So, if all you do is spend your days wanting and missing them, you will attract just that—more days of wanting them and that awful feeling of desperation will never end.

Author Gary Zukav said we must learn not to be in the river of our emotions; we must learn to watch our emotions from above the bridge. We need to get you above the bridge, and the only way to do that, the only way to get you to see the relationship for what it actually was, is to remember that there is another side to this. This brings us to our next exercise.

Dethroning Them: *Kicking Your Ex Off the Pedestal*

This exercise will help you see things from a clearer and more realistic perspective; it will also be freeing and cathartic. It is a hugely important step to help you get out of that lovesick bubble and back into your life. I know you might be hesitating because you are still in love with your ex. But trust me, when you go through this part of the process, you are going to start feeling better because you are going to realize that the reason you are struggling so much is not entirely about losing your ex. This should give you some hope. There are a host of reasons why you are struggling. For many, it's about losing the whole concept of being in a relationship. It's the idea of having invested so much of yourself, of being part of that circle of couples, of finally finding someone and feeling like you don't know who you are without them.

When my ex and I first split, I beat and berated myself about how I could have let this happen. I thought my ex was the "greatest thing since sliced bread." I exaggerated every detail about him in my mind. I thought about only great things, like our relationship being this long and amazing love story with little birds singing in the background, where hardly anything went wrong. I reimagined it as only fulfilling and loving times. In reality, our marriage had been in a rut for a while. We hardly had sex anymore and had very little to talk about other than his music or his band.

But I was so desperate to hold onto my marriage and those seventeen years together that deliberately dismissed any thoughts about the fact that he betrayed me in the worst way possible. He had an affair while I was grieving my little brother's death! In addition, I had forgotten that every weekend and waking moment was consumed with talking about music and his bands and that we couldn't have one conversation about politics or philosophy because those just weren't his interests; and I completely ignored the fact that we were together since we were eighteen and I had put my entire life on hold for him and encouraged his dreams—only to find him having an affair with a woman from the "adult film industry."

Trust me, I don't say this to berate my ex-husband. He is a good guy, and I wish him the very best out of life. I have no regrets about our relationship. The love that we shared when we were younger was real, and nothing will change that. I say this because these are the things that were so important for me to remind myself of in order to gain perspective. I needed to really "see" our relationship without the rose-colored glasses so that I could finally move on and heal. This exercise is one of the things that really helped me finally open my eyes, kick this relationship to the curb, and slam the door forever. It will help you, too.

Okay. Let's get started. Get a piece of paper and the *Best of Alanis Morissette* CD—or Taylor Swift for the younger generation (just kidding). Now, close your eyes. I want you to think only the bad and the ugly things. Focus only on the flaws of the relationship. Think back to all of the things about he/she that pissed you off or made you uncomfortable. Think about any red flags you experienced in this relationship that you just ignored. Think about the fights that you had, and how you gave up X, Y, or Z for him. Exaggerate your feelings so you can really pull them out! Think about all of the ways they did you wrong, all the ways this relationship fell short for *you*. All the ways they disappointed *you*.

Be honest and as specific as you can. This is extremely important for this exercise. It is essentially doing the opposite of what your brain has been doing to process this divorce or breakup. You are going against your brain's psychological bias right now.

Are you ready? Okay, start writing. It can start with something like:

> I can't believe he/she did _____.
> I remember when _____.
> How did I put up with that?
> I did not like it when he/she _____.
> He/she always kept me from _____.
> I put _____ on hold for
> him/her only to _____

Keep it going. Let it all pour out! You get the picture. Let yourself go nuts! You want this to be really charged and pissy! You should feel pretty charged right now.

Next, take this piece of paper and laminate it, if you need to, but keep it with you at all times. Whenever you find yourself on the verge of a breakdown, take it out and read it. Read it out loud if possible and necessary.

By doing this exercise consistently, you will eventually find yourself over the river looking down. You will be able to detach yourself from all of these over embellished fantasy thoughts about your ex and have a more realistic sense of your relationship. You will be off the hamster wheel and on your way to your healing path.

Meditation

Now that you are charged, and are feeling your emotions running through you, you need to calm your state of mind and recenter yourself. Meditation is the most effective and the most valuable technique to do just that. If you have never meditated before, please don't worry. It is a practice that gets better the more you do it, and you can learn to train yourself to clear your mind temporarily, and be present with yourself, your body, and your breath. Whenever you take time to be still, you create a quiet space for awareness and reflection. This will help you feel clearer and more confident with important things throughout your day. With continued practice, you will be able to do this meditation anywhere and at any time. Throughout this book, I will teach you a series of meditations to help you on your journey and reenter yourself. So, let's get started.

Centering Meditation

Sit on a chair, on the floor, or wherever you're most comfortable. Make sure your spine is straight but not rigid. Let it be relaxed. As you begin to settle, relax your shoulders and arms and place your hands on your lap, facing upward or downward, whichever feels more natural.

Now, gently close your eyes and just feel yourself letting go. Trust this moment and surrender to your breath. You are going to take three deep breaths in through your nose and out through your mouth at your own pace.

Next, take a nice, deep breath in through your nose and out through your mouth. Take another deep breath in through your nose and out through your mouth. One more time, in through your nose and out through your mouth—totally emptying out every breath from your belly.

And now, let your breath come naturally. Notice how your breath is flowing. Is it fast and shallow or is it slow and deep? Just notice. Keep letting go. Feel yourself relaxing even more just quieting and clearing your mind from any problems of the day. You will have plenty of time to get to today's tasks, but for this moment, let them go.

Gently push any thought that comes up in a bubble, and just let it go. Just blow it away and release it. You're now in a state of nonresistance, and your vibration is high and pure. So, allow yourself to breathe and relax.

I want you to picture yourself sitting on a chair, and beginning with the top of your head, you're going to gently scan your body for any feelings of tension or stress. Start with your head, your forehead, and your eyes, and then bring your focus to your nose and your mouth. Relax your jaw and your neck. Notice anywhere you feel any tightness, tension, or resistance, and just breathe into that area.

Keep scanning down your chest. Feel your ribs expand with each breath. Go down to your stomach, your arms, your hands, your fingertips, and continue up and down to the bottom of your spine. Gently guide your breath anywhere you feel tightness and release that tightness with your breath.

Continue scanning from your torso, your stomach, your glutes, your pelvic area, your legs, your feet down and down to your toes. Notice if you're feeling any other sensations. Think about anywhere you feel you are carrying the most stress or tension, and breathe into it. Inhale white-light energy, and exhale the negativity and tension.

I want you to picture yourself surrounded by a beautiful golden light. This golden light is soothing and calming and it's enveloping your body like a cocoon. Just sit in this light, in this state of calmness and nonresistance for a few moments. Feel your pureness, and your beautiful vibrations. As you hold yourself in this place for a few more seconds, repeat after me:

> *"I am a strong, amazing person who trusts the universe and the process of life. Everything happens for a reason, and this experience is making me stronger."*

When you are ready, open your eyes. You can look up this meditation on my website www.myselftruly.com for additional reference. For those who have a hard time finding their inner silence or sitting still, no problem. You can follow a guided meditation from wherever you are. There are tons of books, downloads, and even free phone apps that you can use anywhere. My favorite app is Insight

Timer. It's free and has tons of guided and unguided meditations for different lengths of time.

Taking Care of Yourself

You are doing a lot of work, and I commend you for this. You are a rock star! By now, I am sure you are feeling your strength kicking in a little bit. If you haven't already, it is time to start a good self-care regime. Remember that your body and mind are going through a host of changes and adaptation to a new life. It is really important to be gentle with yourself and to nurture yourself. This means eating right, taking vitamins, exercising, and getting some much-needed sleep.

Eat Right

I know that when you are going through heartbreak, you are very depressed, and the last thing you care about is eating, especially eating the right foods. But if you keep in mind that a healthy body can help maintain a healthy mind-set, it is important that you take good care of it right now. This doesn't mean you should avoid eating that pizza and having some wine when you are with your friends or having junk food on a day when you just feel like letting your hair down, but make it a priority to nourish your body and make healthy choices. Remind yourself that your ups and downs will be handled much better when your mind and body are in sync.

Sleep Right

I know you know how important it is to get a good night's sleep. Having good sleeping habits is good for your overall health, and poor sleeping habits are linked to depression. When you sleep, your body and mind really recover. It's kind of like rebooting your system. While you are nursing heartbreak, it is even more important that you try to get that rest. Your entire body is going through a lot. Lack of sleep really affects how you process emotions and function the next day.

Exercise

Exercising has so many upsides, and in times of healing, it is especially beneficial for you. In addition to weight loss, increased strength, better sleep, and all the other amazing health benefits, exercising actually boosts happiness levels and helps you get better at setting and achieving goals. No, you don't need to run a 10k, but getting at least fifteen to thirty minutes a day of exercise will make a huge difference in your life.

Remember, a breakup is comparable to a drug addict going through withdrawals. So why not use that cortisol and adrenaline to get yourself in great shape? I got in the best shape of my life through my divorce. Once I became determined to heal, I made the gym part of my daily life routine. Each day, no matter how bad I felt, I forced myself to go to the gym and get on the treadmill. I always felt stronger and more uplifted afterward. Each time I went it got easier, and watching my body getting stronger and in good shape gave me such a boost of confidence. Next thing I knew, I was doing boot camp and kickboxing classes and going for runs. And I never thought about my ex during my workout time. It was amazing. I was having secret workout contests with myself!

 LET'S RECAP _____

- Release negative emotions with emotional freedom technique (EFT), or tapping.
- Sign the contract to break all contact with your ex
- Gather your "Angels" (your amazing team of friends and family) to support you
- Dethrone your ex and see them in their real light
- Begin a meditation practice
- Start a self-care regime with sleep, exercise, and a sensible diet

In this next chapter, I will guide you through setting intentions and affirmations. I will explain the strength in finding gratitude at this time and how doing small good deeds for others can elevate your state of mind. Keep an open mind and know that I am there with you and holding the highest vision for you.

Chapter 4:

Intentions—Compass for Life

Healing Crystals: Black Agate, Clear Quartz, Brown Agate

You are on a new journey, and I commend you for your strength. You now have ideas and techniques to help you keep strong along the way. You are ready to keep going. This is not the time to be wandering on autopilot, getting frustrated, or giving up. For this reason, we are going to discuss more about setting an intention.

Intention

Deepak Chopra says it most perfectly, "Intention is the starting point of every dream."

Think of an intention like a compass; it helps guide you with a long-term vision for the future by planting a seed in your mind that keeps expanding and growing, like a flower being watered, each time you announce it. It describes what it looks like to already be at the other side of your life, where you have already achieved your goal and whatever it was you were trying to change. An intention helps you manifest what you truly want and stay on course during the process.

When you set an intention, you are declaring to the universe that you are ready to take the next step, kick butt, and get what you want. By having an intention, and reading that intention every day, the universe shows up with people, events, and opportunities that align you with your intention. Without an intention, there is a probability that you will eventually get discouraged, let a self-limiting belief creep up and take over, and you will want to throw in the towel, especially if you have a run in with your ex. We are literally working on reprograming your brain from enculturation and the habits that it is used to doing every day, like thinking about your ex 24/7, to starting new habits that will keep you moving forward. And since your brain is resisting, because it very much wants to get you to go back to your old way of thinking and be unchanging, it is so crucial that you set an intention and understand the power of repetition.

Before you set your intention, it is really important that you are in a positive space. What better way is there to do that than to get in a place of gratitude? So, close your eyes. Take a deep breath in through your nose and out through your mouth. Now, think of something you are grateful for today. As I mentioned before, we all have things to be grateful for, even in times of grief. Reach for that thing you are thankful for right now. Feel your gratitude. Hold onto it for a few seconds. Let it put a smile on your face. Next, put your hand over your heart and say, "Thank you." Now you may open your eyes.

Now it's time to write down your intention. Remember that an intention is a statement stating the result or outcome that you want for your life. It should be one to two sentences long. Here are a few examples:

- I've decided that despite this divorce/breakup, I will keep living an amazing, full and exciting life.
- I love the idea of seeing myself laughing and spending lots of quality time with my friends and family, having this freedom to meet new people, explore new places, and create the best memories.
- I love knowing that I am on an amazing self-discovery journey.
- I am excited at the thought of putting this phase of my life in the past and becoming a fully empowered, thriving woman.
- I am excited to make new beautiful memories.

- I'm excited at the thought of trying things I have never tried before.

Once you have your intention written up, read it out loud to yourself in the mirror. Tape it to your mirror, so you can see it and read it every day. I cannot stress enough that repetition is key to this exercise. So, repeat your intention in the morning after waking up and in the evening before bed.

I have consistently noticed that when I guide my clients through setting intentions, they are visibly hopeful and so excited. One particular client comes to mind. She told me that setting intentions changed her life because it shifted how she approached her goals. The intention that she set during our work together was based on her desire to heal and move on from her breakup. She said that reading her intention out loud in the morning and before bed really kept her motivated and inspired throughout the day to stay on track with the work she was putting in. By having her intention in writing, it was like having a note about her future already in her hands, making it seem so possible and attainable for her.

Affirmations

Whenever we are grieving, whether it's a breakup or divorce, we are often filled with self-limiting beliefs. Self-limiting beliefs will keep you trapped in a state of negative. Affirmations are amazing tools to change these limiting beliefs and lift the negative chatter to keep you on your path to healing.

In one of the beautiful books that I read by Louise Hay called *You Can Heal Your Heart*, she continually talks about challenging your thoughts to change unhealthy patterns. Using affirmations will help you do that. Affirmations are positive, present tense statements that will help you overcome negative thoughts. As you can see, in the previous chapter, I inserted some affirmations in the meditation. You can use affirmations for any situation wherever you are struggling and want to make a change. Affirmations are a perfect tool to use for where you are right now, and when used in conjunction with your Intention, you will have the glue that keeps you grounded on your tracks and moving forward on your healing process.

Creating your own positive affirmations is really simple. To begin, write down a persistent negative thought or self-talk and write down an affirmation that is the opposite of that thought or belief. Phrase it so that it sounds meaningful to you.

The following guidelines will help you get started:

- Always start with the words "I am"
- Use only *present* tense
- Always make a positive statement
- Keep it specific
- Try to include an "–ing" (action) word
- Include a feeling word

A couple of examples of affirmations using these guidelines could be "As I open myself to face my grief, I am healing," or another one could be "I am looking forward to discovering my best self."

Gratitude Journal

No matter what is going on in our lives, even in these times of grief, there is always something to be grateful for. One of the great things I learned while on my own healing journey is that while you are in a place of gratitude, you cannot be angry or sad because gratefulness and anger cannot coexist at the same moment. So, by practicing gratitude, even if it's only for a few seconds, you are already shifting your energy vibrations and by writing these down before bed, you will be going to sleep with a better state of mind.

So, get a notebook or journal to keep next to your bed. Every night before bed, write down three to five things you are grateful for. Don't just write these down; try to really feel the gratefulness as you are writing each one down. While you might not think you can think of anything to be grateful for right now, I promise there are many things to be grateful for, such as:

- I am thankful for waking up
- I am thankful for my health
- I am thankful for the air in my lungs
- I am thankful for my family
- I am thankful for the bed I sleep on

- I am grateful that I have food to eat and water to drink

Do you see what I mean? There are tons of things to be grateful for every day. Tune into them.

On days when I was on the kitchen floor letting my feelings of sorrow go through me and drowning me in tears, there always came a point where I would start to think about third-world countries. There are so many little children around the world who are plagued with war on a daily basis. I thought about stories of some families with little children who lived in holes underground for fear of being killed. This would suddenly stop me in my tracks, help me get my sorry self up, and feel inspired to give sincere gratitude for my life. As miserable as I felt and as much as I thought my life was falling apart (I was going through a freaking divorce), I was not fighting hunger or war. This always helped put things in perspective. It was impossible not to look around and think of a million different things to be grateful for at that moment. I know this may seem a little extreme, but it always worked for me. I would really feel a deep sense of gratitude come over me. Gratitude was basically like the antidote that stopped me from going off the rails and falling into that bottomless well of self-pity and grief.

Doing Small Deeds for Others

Along with setting intentions and affirmations, another way to keep you in a high, positive, motivated, mode is by performing small good deeds every day. Don't worry, I am not talking about anything big. It can be something as little as opening the door for someone, offering a compliment to someone, offering a kind word to someone who is having a rough day, or visiting someone who is lonely.

The idea here is to keep you inspired and open. If you keep this simple exercise as part of your daily routine, you will find yourself in a more positive state, and you will be making someone else smile in the process.

Here a few more examples of good deeds:

- Picking up trash on the sidewalk
- Recycling
- Being someone's shoulder to cry on
- Volunteering at a local soup kitchen
- Reading at a children's school
- Offering prayers for someone, even if it's someone on social media who needs them

In an article from Goodnet.org, "7-Scientific Facts about the Benefits of Doing Good," the writer talks about the sensation known as "helper's high," which is produced when your brain releases endorphins, the feel-good chemicals in the brain. And they talk about how doing good deeds has been known to generate feelings of gratitude. This explains why every time I do something nice for someone, and I see their smile, it always gives me a little jolt of joy and a great feeling in my heart. Pretty soon after I began this ritual, I began doing four to five good deeds a day. It really helped me get out of my divorce funk for a while and make others feel good in the process. So, the next time you are feeling tender, get out and do a good deed for someone. Trust me, you won't regret it!

↻ LET'S RECAP _____

- Understand the power of setting intentions and how to use them in your healing and growth
- Write down positive affirmations to keep you aligned to your intentions and help get rid of self-limiting beliefs or enculturation
- Keep a gratitude journal next to your bed and write down three to five things before going to bed to raise your energy vibrations and help you heal during sleep
- Perform small, good deeds for others to keep you deeply inspired and help others through their struggle

In the next chapter, I will talk about acceptance and how resisting the present will keep you trapped in misery. I will also talk about self-love and the biggest mistakes people make when nursing their heartbreak.

I am so proud of you. You have gotten this far and should already be feeling a shift; even if it's a small change—it's progress. Celebrate by doing something good for yourself. My hope is that the next chapters will help you continue on your healing path feeling more empowered and knowing that the universe is on your side.

Chapter 5:

Acceptance

Healing Crystals: Botswana Agate, Howlite, Lepidolite

My Epiphany Moment

One day, I felt myself having a massive breakdown when I looked into the mirror in complete shock. It had been an extraordinarily bad day. My ex-husband and I had just met with a marriage mediator for the first time, and this was the first time in two weeks I was seeing him after our split. Shortly after, I felt incredibly ill. I was basically crawling on my kitchen floor, sick to my stomach, my body in full pain, even the palms of my hands hurt, and my heart felt completely butchered.

On that day, when I stared at the mirror, I saw nothing left of me. I saw a deflated, broken version of myself. And that was the day that reality sunk in. I suddenly understood that I was letting all of this happen to me. My ex didn't have the power to do this to me. I was responsible for doing this to myself and for my reactions.

For a few seconds, I couldn't believe I had been treating myself so badly. I had been letting myself get stuck in grief and seriously neglecting myself in the process. That was the day that I knew I had to make a choice. Either I had to accept what was happening, try to see even the tiniest positive in it, and choose to get in a peaceful, but strong state of mind somehow, or I could fight, resist, and choose to become more depleted, broken, and miserable and struggle against the universe for the rest of my life. Needless to say, I chose to accept the present and become the creator of my life.

Acceptance is a choice and an opportunity to change your life. When you refuse to accept the present moment and the circumstances around it, you are actually causing yourself more anxiety and stress and essentially straying from the valuable lesson. The Buddhists have a formula: Pain x Resistance = Suffering. In other words, by resisting, and trying to avoid your pain, you are actually causing the reverse outcome. You are clinging on to pain and adding more suffering instead of releasing it.

When your relationship ends, you instantly go into panic mode; your head gets flooded with feelings of desperation and destructive thoughts, and your mind shifts from attacking yourself to attacking your partner. Although this is completely normal, if you are not careful, this can put you on a hamster wheel where vicious, negative thoughts will keep you unable to heal and move forward. You will be flowing with negative energy and with daily thoughts and questions like:

- Who is ever going to love me again?
- Will I ever find anyone like him/her again?
- Now we will never have dinner together again.
- We will never sleep in the same bed together.
- I will never have any children.
- We will never be in a car together again.
- I'm too old. No one is going to find me attractive anymore.
- How could he/she do this to me?
- He/she is the most selfish person on the face of the earth.
- How could he/she betray me this way?
- What is so wrong with me?
- I am broken.
- Do I have anything to offer anyone anymore?
- Will I ever love anyone the same way again?
- Will anyone ever love me again?

These thoughts will likely cause you to want to run or avoid your present, but rather than resist, and add suffering, you must allow yourself to experience what you are struggling with. I don't mean stay in this place the entire day, but rather give yourself periods of time to process the grieving feelings before finding ways to get distracted. This will help you find healthy ways to find comfort and support while releasing some of the pain. It will also help you develop self-compassion and teach you how to be authentic and find inner peace in the long run.

Some people get stuck in denial and pretend that it's not over. This can be especially destructive to your life because you will literally remain paralyzed and never move forward with your life. I have seen many take on drinking, drugs, extra work, sex, and even the gym as a way to keep busy and deny their new reality. This is swimming against the current. Your life will remain a continuous struggle this way.

Look at your situation and realize there is nothing you can do about it. You tried your very best; you did everything you could do, but you cannot change the outcome. Now it's time to let go of the oars and swim with the current, with the flow of the river. Trust me, I am not saying it's easy. I get that you feel resistant to accept this new life, after all, it is extremely frightening and maddening to leave what you know and not know what's ahead. But hiding out and pretending the present is not happening or that it can still change will only add to your pain and the duration of your emotional roller coaster. Stop for a moment and think back to one of those times growing up when you wished for something so bad, but later realized that your parents were right for not letting you have this thing. Or think back to the time you wished a relationship didn't end, but later thanked your lucky stars that you didn't get your wish because it would have been a complete train wreck. Remembering these times can help you see how life, God, or the Universe was preparing you for something better. So it's the same here. When this door closed, know that another door, a much bigger door has opened. It's your job to find that door.

It is important to explore that a lot of the painful, negative feelings you are experiencing have already been there all along and are not solely from your divorce or breakup. There have been past hurts that were internalized all these years and have now been unleashed, like a floodgate, through this traumatic experience.

It is also important that you change your view of relationships. Relationships and marriages are supposed to add to your life experiences and not define who you are as a person. Since childhood, you have been programmed with this beautiful fairy tale of the prince and the princess sharing this tender kiss and living happily ever after. The problem is that this is just a fairy tale. As adults we understand that relationships and marriages are not going to be perfect, but I believe many of us still have a little tiny kid inside of us who is hoping for the perfect story ending. Relationships and marriages take work, and sometimes they end; so just because your marriage is over, it doesn't mean you're inadequate, inferior, or that there's something wrong with you. Sometimes relationships just end. Sometimes your journey together is not meant to be forever, and you need to find a way to accept that and be at peace with it. True happiness comes to you when you have the understanding that life is continuous and ever changing and that you always have a choice. You can get stuck in the current (resistance), or embrace the change, allow and let go of the oars so that you can flow with the river. This is what some call the Law of Allowing. Author and motivational speaker, Dr. Wayne Dyer, continuously gave timeless advice on "allowing." In a nutshell, he said, "You have to just be. You have to let go. You have to allow." And by embracing this heightened level of consciousness, you will find true inner peace and end your suffering.

Self-love

You are a valuable, powerful being who doesn't have to let the end of your love relationship define your self-worth. No person can complete you. You are a whole human being all on your own. Oftentimes, the reason for your intense suffering has a lot to do with the fact that your partner was filling you with an emotional benefit you were not giving yourself.

Let us think about this. If I were to ask you right now what was the biggest emotional benefit you were getting from your ex, what would you say? Journal this.

My ex was always telling me what a good person and great soul I was. At the time, I was not aware I had low self-esteem or that I had self-loathing issues, so being with him made me see myself as worthy and wholesome. So, when he was gone, I felt broken. I felt lost and unworthy, and that was excruciating.

One of my clients discovered through her ex that she had a deep love for art and deep spiritual conversations. Her ex was able to engage her in conversations about the moon and the stars. They talked about poetry and painters and about spirituality and the world. He seemed to connect to her in a way that none of her other partners, friends, or family had ever been able to. She felt understood by him, and she felt free, uncensored, fulfilled, and validated through him. Once he was gone, she felt empty and confused. What she didn't realize, when the relationship ended, was that that whole intense, beautiful, and spiritual person didn't disappear when her ex split. She was still right there. All she had to do was reach inside herself. Once she discovered this, she was able to find there are many like-minded souls out there and that there are actually communities and meetups where she could be herself, express her deep loves, and feel like a whole woman all on her own.

Another client of mine was terrible at setting goals and keeping track of his finances, and his ex was masterful in these areas. She had a degree in finance and accounting and loved setting goals, so he always felt this incredible sense of financial security when they were together. My client was not especially fond of math, so in his mind he had long set self-limiting beliefs around the notion that he was incapable. He didn't think he had the head for setting financial goals. When she was gone, he felt like a complete failure. He started feeling lost about his financial future, and he even started messing up his credit by missing credit card payments and thought without her he would not get ahead.

Once he recognized that these issues came from his own self-limiting beliefs, he was able to change all of this. He realized that all he needed to do was make a few simple calls or look online to get simple answers, and he was able to set solid financial goals afterward. He took charge of his own financial needs without depending on a partner and felt such relief and truly uplifted for it.

Because you never gave yourself these emotional benefits, you have built self-limiting beliefs around them instead, and you are likely suffering so much more then you should. Your ex filled you with certain emotions that you were lacking in yourself, so now that they are gone, you feel vulnerable, inadequate and like there is a void. So, recognize what it is, write this down in your journal, and start to give yourself this missing benefit. If you can't figure out where or how to start, seeking a therapist or a life coach can be really helpful with this.

If you can develop the understanding that nothing is a coincidence, you will see that all of your relationships are assignments. Your relationships did not happen by accident, nor were they mistakes, so you shouldn't regret them. They are here for you to learn about yourself. They give rise to hidden hurts that need your attention. And if you don't stop to see and learn the lesson and choose to run away instead, you will keep repeating the same mistakes over and over again in other relationships, or other aspects of your life.

For example, I have a client who kept falling into the same trap. She kept attracting the same guy in different forms. He had different jobs and different looks but was the same personality (self-centered, controlling, and mentally abusive). She once asked, "I don't understand. Why does this keep happening?" Together, we discovered that on a subconscious level, she had been reliving her relationship with her parents. Her relationship with her parents had been so dysfunctional throughout her life that she was stuck trying to change the ending of her childhood story with the men she dated. But once her floodgates were opened through a painful breakup, she used this opportunity to learn. She allowed herself to be raw and vulnerable. She was able to really see her actions from a whole new perspective, and she was free. She suddenly understood that these guys were indeed lessons. They were there to open past hurts and experiences in order for her to heal. With this knowledge, she was able to break the old patterns. She was off the hamster wheel, and she found her beautiful self, her authentic self.

Biggest Mistakes People Make While Going through a Breakup

You are not what happened to you.

A person whose marriage or relationship has ended due to their partner's doing, must fight against falling prey to a victim mentality. This is where you blame your ex for your happiness being taken away while giving yourself permission to make irresponsible choices or take on dangerous habits and behavior while taking no accountability or responsibility for them once they draw serious consequences.

One example of such behavior is a person who goes on a sex rampage with several people, usually strangers, has unprotected sex, and contracts a disease as a consequence. Another example is a person who starts drinking heavily or doing drugs, ends up losing his or her job or, worse, hurting or killing someone.

There are many ways a victim mentality can destroy your life and cause you to lose your close friends. Even if you don't take on these dangerous behaviors, you can also alienate yourself from your friends and family if you develop a consistent, draining, or overwhelming "poor me" attitude long after your relationship has ended. Please don't misunderstand, grieving the loss of your marriage and sharing your pain with loved ones is a completely normal and healthy part of your healing; however, getting stuck there for years and becoming an emotional vampire is not.

I have met a few people over the years who are stuck in this victim mentality and whom others shy away from. A particular client comes to mind because he came to me when he had lost all of his close friends and noticed that even relatives were not returning his calls so often. He couldn't understand what happened and blamed everyone, especially his ex-wife, for how his life was unfolding. I quickly picked up from his language that he was operating under this victim-mentality mode. He was completely stuck in the past and only relived happy moments that involved his ex-wife. He later realized this was the reason why everyone was turning away from him. He was later told that they were tired of the old repetitive stories, especially because it was frustrating to watch him be stuck in a time warp. Someone explained that he used to be such a fun guy to be around but had developed this dark cloud over him ever since he and his ex-wife split years back and that he drained everyone with all of his complaints.

Learning to identify when it's time to persist and when it's time to let go and accept is crucial to healing and growing and sometimes letting go and closing the door is the only way.

Breakup Traps

There are also other things that you need to be mindful of while grieving the loss of a loved one. I call these breakup traps. Breakup traps show up in the following ways:

Jumping Right into Another Relationship

The fear of being alone or wanting to fill the space an ex held can be so strong that many try to jump right into another relationship. When you are on your own again, it is normal for you to feel a sort of desperation to fill that void. Some even go as far as getting married again, shortly after. But you must refrain from falling into this trap. Several things can come from following this path, and none of them are good.

- You are so vulnerable that you will attract a wrong someone who will prey on your weakness
- You will settle for a person completely wrong for you
- You will carry all of the hurt and baggage from your marriage into this relationship, and ruin it
- You will make the same exact mistakes, or worse mistakes, as your previous relationship
- You will waste the wonderful opportunity to learn about yourself
- You will try to make them into your ex, and they will hate you for it, or you will lose the desire to be with them once it wears off

Remember, you are raw, emotional, and brokenhearted after your marriage or relationship has ended. You are in no way, shape, or form ready to attempt a new relationship right now. Getting into another relationship again without working through the painful emotions is like putting a bandage on a hemorrhaging wound. And when we seek validation and safety in another in order to feel whole again, eventually you will become unfulfilled and start to feel the intense void creep up again. You may start to act out in undesirable ways to your new partner or want to isolate yourself. It will not only be unfair and unsafe for you to attempt another relationship right now, but it will be unfair to someone who may deeply care about you.

Running from the Pain with Alcohol or Drugs

I know it hurts. It feels like torture to lose someone you loved and shared a life with. It is very easy to want to quiet or numb that pain. You just want it to go away, so you might start drinking, doing drugs, or submerging yourself in your work. We have all heard that quote "what we resist persists." It doesn't matter if you run, the problems will always be there, sometimes manifesting in different forms and in different areas of your life, so why not face them head on so you can release them?

I know many people who have lived so much of their lives running from pain by using alcohol or drugs. This has, at many times, put them in irresponsible or dangerous positions, such as having irresponsible sex, getting black-out drunk, getting a DUI, catching a venereal disease, or much worse. Think very carefully before you act out on your pain. As we discussed earlier, have your Angel Team ready on speed dial to support you. It is not worth going down this road ever.

Never Dating Again

Although this sounds like it's a better alternative, in reality, this is just another way of hiding out or running away. Deciding to take yourself completely off the market and never date again so you don't have to experience pain is just plainly robbing yourself from living. Learning to be on your own and becoming self-reliant is awesome and a wonderful way to move forward, but becoming a hermit or doing things to ensure that you never have time for dating is in fact another method for running away. And in turn, you will not truly heal. Furthermore, you will miss out on the wonderful experience of getting to know yourself again and seeing how much fun it is to have a partner to enhance your life. This is not to say that choosing to be alone is wrong. Making the choice to be alone once you have gone through the process of healing is a completely different thing.

One of my sisters-in-law went through a difficult divorce many years ago. She dated guys here and there since, and got in a relationship but nothing really worth it. Although she is single, she has no regrets about it. She is extremely proud to have raised four beautiful children who are doing amazing, and she feels thrilled about her life and has been enjoying getting to know herself on a deeper level throughout the years.

Some might find that, although they are not completely closing off the possibility of romance, they are so enthralled by what they are finding out about themselves and feel so happy to finally be embracing who they are, that they just want to continue diving in and be alone to continue peeling back more layers. Being on a self-discovery mission can be really riveting and fulfilling and, for some, the love that they discover for themselves is enough.

C LET'S RECAP

- Acceptance is a choice and a great opportunity to change your life. By refusing to accept the present circumstances, you are actually causing yourself more pain, anxiety and stress and ultimately delaying your healing process.

- You are not what happened to you. Stay clear from the victim mentality, which will keep you trapped and unable to move forward.

- Find that emotional benefit that you were getting from your ex, and learn how to give it to yourself.

- Beware of the breakup traps and how they can affect not only you but others as well.

Relationships challenge us and make us grow. They come up to show us the parts of ourselves that have been left unhealed so that we can begin to work on them. Don't allow yourself to become paralyzed with fear from your current circumstances. There is so much to learn from this experience and so much goodness waiting on the other side.

Chapter 6:

Self-Awareness—Time Alone a New Best Friend

Healing Crystals: Amazonite, Aventurine, Golden Obsidian

For about a year after my ex-husband and I split up, I became pretty self-destructive. I anesthetized myself with dating tons of men, most of who were ten years younger than me. I also used alcohol, cigarettes, and the gym as numbing agents. I thought if I could keep myself super busy and keep my mind from going "there," time would heal me. I tried to convince myself that the healing would somehow happen while I was distracted. This was all a fantasy. Time does not heal all. Pain that is not faced will not go away. You have to put in the work and resolve it, if not, you will carry it into the future with you. I later came to realize that time alone by myself was an amazing opportunity to get all of the gunk, all of the self-loathing, and old hurts out of me. It was an amazing time to get to know myself at my core and learn to love myself in a way I never did before.

Even if you think you know yourself pretty well, think about how much you have changed since the last time you were single. Things are not the same. You are not the same person you were then. Going through a broken heart allows you to see yourself in a different light and helps you to grow as a person. This time, this window, can help prepare you for who you are meant to be as a person, and in turn, you will learn who is really compatible with you and who is truly worthy of you.

If you are like many people I know, you seldom take the time to look within yourself, so there is much to discover. This is the time for you to go exploring and for self-introspection. If you skip it this time, you will miss out on a gigantic opportunity to become the best version of yourself. You will miss out on seeing your true self and making the positive changes to your life that will align you with your truest self and live the life you deserve.

You've heard that quote "it's always darkest before dawn." It took this divorce for me to really understand what this quote really meant. It took a long time for me to understand that this explosion, this opening of the floodgates needed to happen for me to change my life. I was so closed-minded and in denial about so much, that my world had to collapse for it to be rebuilt from the bottom up. I had been stuffing and bottling up so much pain and resentment for too long, that it was time. This divorce gave me that time. I was able to take the space that I desperately needed to bloom, to grow, to heal so I could be who I was meant to be. Once I realized that all of my post-divorce, dysfunctional behaviors were hindering my healing and growth, and prolonging my pain, I decided to stop and look for a different path. I ditched all of my senseless dating and partying and took about a year and a half to be by myself. This year and a half was the most amazing and enlightening time of my life.

So many things came to light during this time. I realized that dating these twenty-five-year-old guys was just my way of making myself feel better because my self-esteem was down in the gutter. All of my partying behavior with friends was also just numbing me temporarily and hurting me because it was keeping me from healing. These behaviors were like trying to put a bandage on a really deep wound. It was never going to make anything better; eventually the bandage was going to fall off and the walls of my hideout were going to collapse.

When I took this time off, so many amazing things happened in my life. I became so much closer to my family and friends. I was able to appreciate conversations with them, listen to their points of view, even if I disagreed with them. I would take their advice under consideration, which prior to this event, my ego always prevented me from doing. And I was able to speak authentically from my heart about life, spirituality, and similar topics, all things that I would have been too embarrassed to discuss in the past because I always feared being wrong or judged.

But I believe that the most amazing transformation that happened was with my parents. I was, for the first time in my life, able to divulge past hurts and traumatic experiences growing up as a child, which ended up being unbelievably cathartic. I was able to have the most amazing and deepest conversations with both my parents about everything in life. I was able to weep years of pain in my mother's arms, which, in my mind, had never been a possibility. I always felt that I had to pretend to be so strong and so emotionally independent from my parents that I missed out on the hugs and comforting after being hurt. This was a monumental event in my life. I finally understood what people meant when they said there is nothing like going to Mommy when you have a boo-boo.

I became so much more productive at work, because I was able to focus again. I also went from being Ms. Judgmental to trying to bring love, spirituality, and compassion to my work. In a nutshell, I became much more appreciative of those around me and learned to become empathetic.

While on my year break, I also experienced many moments of magic. I watched the most unbelievable sunsets. I drove to the beach every weekend at 4:00 a.m.

to watch the sunrise and listen to the waves crash. I found parks with beautiful trees where I would go and sit with my book and music and just melt into my surroundings. I noticed flowers, trees, and clouds in a way that I had never noticed before. I let myself get caught in the rain a few times and laughed it off while it drenched me. I also discovered that I was, indeed, a very compassionate and giving person.

I started rekindling old habits that I had forgotten about like writing poetry, listening to classical music, and reconnecting with my spirituality. I became enthralled about diving into myself with self-help books. The best part of my solitude was finding myself in it, and I never felt alone! I always felt my surroundings. I had found my home; I found my deepest spirituality. I felt wonderful! I felt different. I felt empowered in every sense of the word. I learned to look at everything with love.

Once I made the conscious choice to stop all of my senseless, destructive behavior, and seek a healthier approach, I learned so much about humility and humbleness. But, I also felt deeply empowered and renewed. This was my first step on my healing path, and I knew that I was going to be just fine. I was better than fine. I found myself and learned to love myself deeply, and I felt so inspired that I began to write poetry again on a daily basis. Here is a poem that I wrote while on my healing path:

Deep within Deep
Silence has brought out the music from within me
Solitude has opened up a door to my soul
I have lived under the whip of fear for too long
Never learning how to walk alone
I have followed the empty promises of society
I have chased other people's dreams as if my own
But among the midst of sudden calmness and sobriety
And deep within the walls of my unknown
I have stumbled into a deep well
A well so deep, it echoes with a thousand songs
As my spirit wishes to be truly seen
And my soul welcomes a lifetime of growth
I must deter my heart from those who have not found
their own wells
Those who have not found themselves on a journey
Those who have not let themselves become unveiled
Those who have never been defeated and then become
victorious
Those who have not taken the road less traveled
Those who have not walked barefoot and felt glorious
Those who play the safe card and never walk into the
unknown
For I have fought too many wars
Endured too many heartaches
Crossed too many rivers
Walked through many treacherous roads
For I have conquered too many battles
Found myself disempowered

Plummeted into many regrets
And found wisdom in my many mistakes
My pilgrimage has been too great and too costly
For me to surrender my heart to the sparkle of lights
Or to the sound of someone else's melody.

– C. Silvestro

Try to be openminded, and remember that getting to know who you are and what you want takes time and patience, and there is no better investment than investing in yourself. Whenever you feel like you are going off your path, return by tapping into your desire to truly heal and to truly get to know yourself with a quick breathing meditation.

Simple Breathing Exercise
- I'd like you to take a deep breath in through your nose and out through your mouth and place your feet flat on the floor. *Feel* the sensation of your feet touching the ground underneath you.
- Now take two to three deep breaths, noticing your stomach rising and falling with each in and out breath.
- And when you feel comfortable, close your eyes.
- Now, as you keep breathing deeply into your stomach, I'd like you to breathe in for a count of five, then hold your breath for a count of five, and breathe out slowly for a count of five. And keep

breathing, in for five, hold for five, out for five. Do this two more times.

- And now, I'd like you to now slowly bring your attention back to the room, noticing the sounds around you and begin to open your eyes.

Take this opportunity to learn and develop an open mind. Let's get an honest look at the real you. Let's begin with a self-awareness check. Journal your current perception of yourself. Think about what you are good at, and what you need improvement on. Think about things that you are proud of, any accomplishments throughout your life.

Perform daily self-reflection. Try and take five to ten minutes a day to journal your thoughts and encourage others to be honest about you. This brings me to my next exercise. This exercise really opened my eyes to so much of my personality that I had never explored before. We often think we know ourselves, but without some help from outside input, we seldom do. With this exercise, you will really begin to know another side of your personality.

The Johari Window

The Johari window was developed by psychologists Joseph Luft and Harry Ingham to help people better understand their relationship with themselves and others. The window consists of four panes representing the four areas of your personality.

1. Only You Know	2. You Show Others
This is the part of yourself that only you know.	This is how you portray yourself to others; the part that you chose to show.
3. Only Others Know	**4. No One Knows**
This is the part of yourself that you are unaware exists, but others can see.	This is the part of yourself that no one knows (not yourself or others).

Quadrant 1

This is the very private and vulnerable part of you that you do not want anyone to see. You have fears and doubts and embarrassing or painful events in here. Only you can see this.

Quadrant 2

This is the part of your personality that you feel secure, safe, and confident with. This is the part that you like to show others. Some you show more than others depending on your trust or comfort level.

Quadrant 3

This is the part that holds things such as your bad habits or other information you are unaware of, such as rolling your eyes when someone annoys you. This can also contain the good habits or traits and the potential that you don't see in yourself.

Quadrant 4

This holds knowledge or potential that you have yet to discover and no one knows, not even you. This quadrant is also where dreams become reality; new thoughts, creativity, and theories are made here. It is the unknown part of you. Some things will be discovered, some never will.

Okay, are you ready?

Step 1

Take a blank piece of paper and use the following words as headings. Underneath each heading, list at least ten words, positive and negative, that describe you in each of the areas of your personality. Don't worry; this is for your eyes only.

- Looks/Appearance
- Temperament
- Personality
- Good/Bad Behavior
- Philosophy/Outlook on Life
- Overall Person

Step 2

Make another copy of these same headings and, this time, do them as you believe *others* see you.

Step 3

Chose five people, friends, relatives or coworkers who you associate yourself with and one close friend. Tell your close friend that you are doing this self-growth exercise and ask if he/she would assist you in this step. Using a spreadsheet, make copies of the same headings and leave the spaces blank for others to fill in at least ten words or phrases for each about how they see you. Put each sheet in envelopes addressed to the five people you chose for this exercise, along with stamped return envelops using your close friend's address. You definitely want to reach out to the people you chose in advance and let them know to expect this. They are not to put their name on them since this is going to be anonymous.

Lastly, let your close friend know that once she gets the letters, she needs to combine the answers into one spreadsheet (she can destroy the letters after). After you receive the spreadsheet from her, take time alone to review the results. Remember, this exercise is meant to show you how others view you, so it is important to remember that they are not meant to hurt or upset you but are just honest thoughts and opinions.

Take a look at the answers. Are you shocked? Surprised? Journal your thoughts about this. Compare this to the two lists you previously completed. Were the answers from others similar to what you wrote? Did they know you better then you thought? Are the answers what you expected? Take notes of the similarities.

Now take note of the traits that did match what you wrote. These are definitely part of who you are and these answer Quadrant 2. Anything else from the spreadsheet answers Quadrant 3. These are things you didn't know about yourself.

After reviewing the three pages, take time to feel good about the nice things you learned about yourself. Think about the ones that you do not agree with or favor. Could any of these traits inhibit your healing goal or your future in general? Make note of these, and turn them into positives with affirmations. We discussed earlier about positive affirmations; this is another great time to use affirmations to reprogram yourself. For example, if others said I am aloof, my new programming could be: "I am a friendly person who tries to make others feel comfortable."

Another example is if others said I am frail, my new programing could be: "I am a strong vibrant woman who doesn't let obstacles stop me."

Take your time. Remember, you don't need to work on everything at once. Once you have your affirmations for your new programming, tape them somewhere you will see them each morning and at bedtime. I always prefer my bathroom mirror. Repetition is key. Make it a point to read your affirmations when you first wake up and before you go to sleep. Do not remove these until they have become part of you, of your thinking, and of your actions.

Along with the Johari window exercise there are other personality and psychometric tests that you can look up and try for free online. If you want to go further, give them a try.

Writing a Personal Letter to Yourself

Writing a letter to yourself is a way to journal your feelings, mark you progress, and mark your milestones. Don't worry if you had a setback before. Remember, healing from a broken heart is not linear. You will likely have ups and downs. The important thing is that you keep getting up and moving forward.

So, let's get started. Write your name, date, your age, and describe yourself and your situation. What has been going on? How are you feeling about things? Remember, this is solely for you, so be honest. At the end, thank yourself for being brave, strong, taking this time to work on yourself, and for facing your emotions head on. Make sure to honor and congratulate yourself on how far you have come. You might want to write a small affirmation at the end. Keep this letter. It will be amazing to look back and read it a year from now or even a few months from now.

In the beginning of this book, we talked about staying away from places and people that remind you of your ex. Assuming that you have been putting in all of your work, it's time you quit avoiding these places and people, and make new memories. It is very freeing to visit a restaurant or visit a place with friends or family and have that become your new memory. My ex-husband and I used to frequent a lot of restaurants and bars. So when I dated my boyfriend, now husband, some of these places came across our path. He always sweetly asked if I would rather go somewhere else, but my reply was always "no way." This was the chance to make new memories with my new love.

So we would go, have a great time, and create new and happy memories. I no longer thought about my ex when I entered these places. It was freeing.

Make a Bucket List

Remember all of those things you wanted to do but your ex had no interest in doing? Or all of the things you thought you could never possibly do or never bothered to try because you thought they weren't "your cup of tea"? Make a list of these. This will be a fantastic way for you to try new things that you might love. Focus on new goals, and not just important goals, but also really fun and exciting things!

For example, fixing your credit is a good thing to put on your bucket list, but skydiving or scuba diving can also be on there, too! The point is to step outside of your comfort zone and explore. You will be amazed about how many things you end up taking in as part of your life.

 LET'S RECAP _____

- Embrace this time alone as a gift to excel you to your highest, most authentic self
- Understand that many things have changed, including you, and now it's the time to go on a self-exploration tour
- Open your mind to some awesome exercises, such as the Johari window, that will help you on your self-discovery journey

- Journal your progress and nurture yourself by writing yourself a letter
- Don't shy away from places that you and your ex visited; make new memories
- Make a bucket list by stepping out of your comfort zone and trying new things, and you will discover that there is so much more to you then you knew

Remember that the best relationship you can nurture right now is the relationship that you have with yourself. Self-awareness is a vital step for this and for taking back control of your life. It allows you to acknowledge without judgment and make any necessary changes to get you to the life of your dreams. You are likely already finding that there is so much more to you then you realized and that you are so much more valuable then you ever acknowledged. Let's keep this going. I am so excited for you!

Chapter 7:

I Forgive You and I Release You

Healing Crystals: Tiger Eye, Peridot, Black Matte

Forgiveness and letting go requires empathy, compassion, kindness, and understanding. It is also a choice. Many times people get stuck in the negative and therefore have a very difficult time forgiving. Whatever your partner did or whatever you think you did that ended the relationship, in order for you to truly heal and move on, you must learn to forgive.

This will be really hard to hear. I explained this to my loved ones while I was in the middle of my divorce debacle, and it was really hard for them to hear and accept. So, please be open-minded and challenge yourself to tap into your compassionate side when you listen to what I am about to say.

This divorce wasn't an easy or sudden move by your ex. This was probably going on in their head for a long time. They probably really wanted to work it out, so they kept putting this off, but eventually the pain of being in this relationship and trying to "suck it up" for the sake of staying together, got to be much worse than whatever was on the other side. No one gets into a relationship or gets married thinking they are going to get divorced someday. You both go into it with the best intentions, the best hopes and wishes, and the best thoughts about the future of your relationship.

Whatever the reason was for the split, you need to remember that this wasn't easy for them either. They probably spent a long time agonizing over this move. They might have even attempted this before but failed because it was too hard or too scary and would be such a significant life change. Remember that they also lost a friend, a lover, and a companion—someone who was part of future plans, vacations, and milestones in their life. Please understand that I don't say this to excuse them in any way. I just want you to try to be empathetic and put yourself in their head. This will help you when you are trying to forgive and let go.

Understanding that my ex's affair was not a direct act to hurt me personally, that it was never an attack to devastate my life, and seeing this with empathetic eyes, knowing that he was suffering too, really helped me. It saved me. Although, some of my friends and family did not agree and thought I was letting him off the hook, I knew exactly what I was doing. I was operating with integrity, compassion, and love. This was what saved my sanity. I knew that this was going to help me to move on, and it did.

Right or wrong, their leaving you was an act of self-preservation. They were trying to take their own pain away. And yes, it was selfish and even cowardly, but once you get through to the other side, you will discover that this was actually a gift to you—gift, wrapped in the crappiest paper, yes, but truly the most amazing gift you can ever receive. If you lean in and do the work, you will see it.

Letting Go Letter

I Forgive You. I Apologize

When my ex and I finalized our divorce, I was still engulfed in emotions of disappointment over not receiving an apology from him and my own guilt over the things that I had done to contribute to our marriage's demise. I couldn't stop the ongoing thoughts. A therapist suggested that I write him a letter. Although I did not receive an apology from him, I chose to write him a letter. I needed to let go, and this was my way of making peace with what happened.

In the letter, I took responsibility for my emotions and for the things that I had done wrong. I listed every single thing that I remembered doing that I knew hurt him, and I told him how it must have made him feel. I apologized for each thing and ended it by telling him that I forgave him for what he had done, that I loved him, and that no matter what, I was grateful that we happened and grateful for our time together. For me, writing this letter was amazingly healing and liberating. It was like a house had been lifted off me.

Sometimes people feel stuck or feel like they can't let go because they have not received an apology from their ex. If that's the case for you, it might help to understand that for some people, saying I'm sorry and admitting they did something wrong is impossible, even if they know down to their core that they wronged the other person. An apology can be extremely difficult to give, especially if it triggers feelings of inadequacy and shame, or if it threatens to tear down the narrative that they constructed for themselves in order to justify and carry out their behavior. Furthermore, if they already have a damaged or warped view of themselves, an apology will likely cause a complete annihilation of their self-worth, and it's just not worth it. Although, yes, you absolutely deserve an apology, it is possible that you will never get one, and sometimes it's better to just give yourself closure and forgive without an apology.

You can start your letter with "I forgive you," list the things that you are forgiving them for, and end it with "I am grateful for our time together."

An apology is like a much-needed gift. It makes you feel deeply understood and validated, so it's understandable to feel the need and craving for one. But if you can't let go from not receiving it, you might want to consider forgiving on your own and doing things to provide yourself the kindness, compassion, and validation you crave.

Go deeper with EFT—tapping exercise from Chapter 4—to continue to release the negative emotions. Write the "I Forgive You" letter mentioned previously, and continue to meditate and nurture yourself. The following is a mindfulness breathing meditation that will help activate the calm space in you and keep your general stress at lower levels throughout the process. The more I have been using these tools and putting mindfulness into my life practice, the more I understand that trusting and knowing that my pain is justified helps me to accept and let go, and I can heal myself independently without an apology.

Breathing Meditation

Gently close your eyes.

Choose an area of the body in which you feel your breath the most.

It could be your chest, your belly, your nostrils, etc.

Now just notice the sensations of breathing

Feel the expansion of your chest as you breathe

Feel your belly moving. Feel it rising on the in-breath and contracting on the out-breath.

Do this several times.

Just notice the sensations for a few minutes.

Even if your relationship ended years ago, it is never too late to write this letter. It might be just the thing that you need to say goodbye to those pesky old ghosts that trigger you every so often.

"Thank you for our time together."

"I am grateful for the lessons I have learned from our relationship."

"I am letting go now."

However it comes up for you, write it, read it to a friend, a coach, or a therapist, so you can feel the act as if you were reading it out loud to them, and then burn the letter. You will feel a sense of peace come over you, a sense of closure, and a knowing that you will be okay. If you feel a little sadness come over you after this, know that it's perfectly normal, just allow it to go through you. Remember, you are still healing. If you still have other items left over like pictures or letters from your ex that you held back in the beginning, this would be a good time to get rid of them too. You can do what I did and perform a burning ceremony afterward.

Because fire is a powerful symbol of purification, a burning ceremony can be very significant in this case and can serve as a ritual to help cleanse and let go. It can help to get rid of the hurt and negative energy you carry from your ex. You can perform this alone or with loved ones for support.

Find a good open space since you will be burning items. Gather music CDs, an old T-shirt of theirs that you might have kept and wear to bed, pictures, letters, and anything that has attachment to them. Make sure you are outside with something large enough, and unburnable where you can put these items. Please be safe and mindful of your surroundings!

Now set an intention such as:

I let go of what no longer serves me.
I accept so that I can be at peace.
I forgive you and let you go.

Make sure you are clear with your intentions and write them down. Stand with both feet planted on the ground. Perform a quick centering or breathing meditation like the one you learned earlier. Let whatever tension and negativity pass through you. Honor yourself for your courage and commitment to let go of all attachment and for being on this healing path.

Now write down what you are letting go of and toss it into the fire. Watch it burn, close your eyes, and take a nice deep breath. Toss whatever other items you have collected and watch them burn. Imagine as the flames are burning that they are getting rid of any negative energy from your past. Feel yourself letting go with the burning items. Feel yourself become free. Journal this experience.

Another one of my favorite rituals is to smudge or burn sage. Light the end of a white sage bundle (you can get it at most stores or online), and blow it out quickly. Walk around your whole house with it or wherever you feel you want to cleanse or release old energy. Let the thick smoke linger, and let it burn down on a safe ceramic bowl or shell.

Choose whatever practice or ritual you want, but remember to be safe and careful. Be gentle with yourself. If you don't feel like you are ready to do this step, it's okay. Take your time. You will get there.

Forgiving is very freeing, but it is a choice, and sometimes it doesn't happen in one swoop. You might hear loved ones tell you to just let go and forgive right away, but in reality, much like grief, forgiveness is not linear; it has phases.

And, as I mentioned earlier, other hurts might come up during these exercises, like things from your past and from others who have wounded you. It's a great idea to write a letter to anyone else who might have hurt you and perform any of the rituals if they helped you before. Get it all out. Sometimes, just putting these things down on paper can help release the old energy.

Forgiveness Meditation

Sit comfortable in a chair or lie down and gently close your eyes

Relax the muscles in your body, one by one

With your eyes closed, gently smile without parting your lips for a few seconds

Now focus on your breath

Gently breathe in through your nose for four counts

Exhale gently through your nose for four counts

Now continue breathing naturally and noticing your breath for two minutes.

While you are relaxed and focused on your breath, begin this series of mantras to remind yourself of your spiritual and loving nature.

On your inhale: I am a spiritual being

On your exhale: I am filled with love

On your inhale: I am one with spirit

On your exhale: I love freely

On your inhale: I honor myself

On your exhale: As I honor others

Visualize the person you want to forgive now.

You are meeting them on a higher, spiritual plane.

See this person in the most positive light. Perhaps they are wearing white, as a sign of purity.

Picture yourself the same way.

Walk slowly to this person and whisper in their ear, "I forgive you."

Continue to talk to the person using only loving words.

"I wish you love and happiness."

"I offer love and forgiveness."

"I offer you peace."

"I thank you for our time together."

Keep talking to this person until you start to feel a release.

Begin saying goodbye.
With extending hands say "My peace I give you."
Now let the visualization fade away slowly.
Begin to bring the focus on your breath.
Breathe in gently through your nose
Breathe out gently through your mouth
Sit comfortably for another few minutes
When you are ready, slowly open your eyes.

LET'S RECAP

Forgiving is liberating but requires your conscious choice. It can be difficult because it requires empathy, kindness, and understanding. But when you are ready, it will be the gift that can transform your life.

Write a forgiveness letter and feel yourself on the path of real love and compassion

Begin rituals to help you with the letting go process and know that these might need to be performed a few times.

The only way for forgiveness to authentically happen is if you work through your pain and emotions. Even after you do these exercises, you might not feel 100 percent done with this phase, and that is perfectly okay. Just know you will get there. You can do this.

Chapter 8:

Rewrite Your Story and Change the Paradigm

Healing Crystals: Carnelian, Bronzite, Rose Quartz

We previously talked about the void left behind and the emotional benefits (emotions or feelings you felt you could only get from your ex), which made you emotionally addicted to them. It's time to ditch that void, by giving yourself that feeling, that emotional benefit, and seeing your full potential so you can soar in your amazing new life.

You have turned the page. This is a new chapter, and adding new daily rituals to your life will help you to manifest your deepest desires. Some of the techniques I have shared with you have helped me really dive inward. They have helped me reach for my dreams and desires. They stem from what is known as the Law of Attraction.

As you'll remember from a previous chapter, the Law of Attraction in a nutshell is "like attracts like," or what you keep your focus on, and the emotions behind these thoughts, brings more of the same to into your life. So envision your life, as you have always wanted it. Really see it and feel the emotions from your thoughts. Write them down and hold this vision.

Visualization

Take five minutes a day and go somewhere you know you will not be disturbed, and close your eyes. Picture that your goal has already happened. You are here. You are healed. Picture what your life is like without the constant pain, anxiety, and obsessive thoughts about your ex. Really visualize what this is like and that it has happened.

What you are doing?

How you are feeling?

Where are you?

What has transpired in your life?

Get as vivid as possible.

Make this a daily practice in the morning before you start your day. It will become the anchor to your healing path.

Self-Introspection: Time for a Self-Inventory

I remember once while on a date, my guy asked me if I would go on a hike with him. My instant response was "that's not really my thing." And right after I stated this, I remember thinking to myself, *Why am I saying that? I have never even tried it. I love nature, so why wouldn't I try it?* I realized when I got home that this was my old programming thinking and talking. The old Carmen thought about how she might break a nail or how her hair might not look good. This shallow, old way of thinking was not serving my highest good, so I needed to ditch this old thinking. Needleless to say, hiking to this day has become one of my favorite hobbies. It is an amazing, therapeutic activity that I will be doing for the rest of my life.

I realized at that moment that I needed to do an internal inventory check. I needed to dive into myself and analyze what else I had been putting these types of self-limiting beliefs on. I went on a quest to see what else I wanted to explore. It was amazing! It turned out I am a bit of a dare devil: I went sky diving and zip-lining a bunch of times, I tried every roller coaster known to man (and didn't like any of them!), and I discovered how much I love doing physically challenging activities, traveling to culturally diverse countries, and exploring the jungle and archaeological sites. And I am still not done.

From that moment, I set out to inventory the most important parts of my life, my career, spirituality, relationships, and so on, and I was able to become crystal clear on what I wanted and was able to put together goals and intentions to get me what I desired.

Now let's do an inventory of the four most important parts of your life: home, career, relationships, and spirituality (or edit these however you see fit), and begin to define the wants and don't wants in these areas to help you become more clear and focused and begin setting goals and intentions to manifesting what you want.

Wants and Don't Wants (*based on a process from* The Law of Attraction *by Michael Losier)*

On a piece of paper, make two columns and write the words "I Don't Want" on the left side, and the words "I Want" on the right column. Now list all of the things you don't like about a specific situation that you are in (from one of the four areas of your life) on the "I Don't Want" side. Once finished, read each line and ask yourself, "What do I want instead?" Cross off the left line and write these answers on the "I Want" side. This very simple exercise helps you really identify what you want and helps you set your intention for how you want to move on with your goals. In the table below is an example of what your "wants" and "don't wants" lists could look like if you were discussing relationships or career.

I Don't Want	I Want
I don't know how to be alone.	I want to feel empowered and excited for my new journey.
I don't want to be home all the time.	I want to fill up my calendar with fun dates with my friends and family.
I am afraid to try things on my own.	I want to enjoy being adventurous and trying all kinds of new activities.

Or if you are choosing career as your topic:

I don't want long hours.	I want to make my own flexible hours.
I don't want to make a small paycheck.	I want to be financially abundant and have enough money to travel and splurge on myself once in a while.
I don't want a boring job.	I want a fulfilling career that makes me feel passionate and excited to go to work.

Once you are done with this list, go down each line on your "want" column and ask yourself, *How do I want to feel?* Make a note of these as well.

Follow your completed list with a positive affirmation statement that combines your wants into one paragraph. For example, using the first example, from a relationship perspective, it would be something like:

"I feel so excited and empowered on my new journey. I fill up my calendar with fun dates with friends and family while having downtime to nurture myself. I enjoy being so adventurous and trying all kinds of new and exciting activities that keep me on my toes."

Make sure that you do one subject at a time. The idea is to express and bring out your desires in a juicy and exciting way. This will raise your vibrations, and keep you on a positive note, which will subconsciously begin turning the wheels in your mind to begin aligning you to your desires. When you are finished, print it and keep it on your nightstand or wherever you will see it and can read it daily.

Altruism

While I was in the midst of my divorce, my dearest friend, Carol, suggested that I think about getting involved in a charity as a way of taking the focus off my pain and giving back. I immediately joined Heifer International, an organization that fights poverty and hunger in many countries around the world, and I felt a sense of hope and compassion come over me. I later joined other charities and became involved in other groups that gave back to the world, such as clean-up groups, hunger and disease walks, and similar. It has become part of my life since then, and I have the deepest respect and admiration for these groups and charities.

If you are where I was back then, and don't have any disposable income to contribute, you can sell items that you don't need, or ask for a small donation (such as the cost of a cup of coffee) from family and friends, or if this seems like too much, you can contribute with a little bit of time. You can go to your local soup kitchen, plant a tree, or read a book to children at one of the local schools in your area. There are so many ways you can contribute without money. Being part of one of these charities or events helps shift the focus off you and onto others who desperately need your help. Through your altruistic acts, you release stress, feel stronger, and have a sense of a much deeper purpose. According to Harvard University studies, "There is evidence that altruistic love may activate certain aspects of the relaxation response" and have a lot of other benefits.

The "Is" Box

Now that you are more excited and hopeful about your future, it's time to get an "Is" box. Unlike a "hope chest," where young ladies kept things in anticipation of marriage, an "Is" box is a beautiful box where you will put all of your dreams and things you are going to manifest. They can be things about love or about your dream career or anything that makes you smile and makes you feel joy when you think about it. It can be a box you already have, or you can pick one up at your local home store. Make sure it feels special to you.

Inside this box you are going to put intentions, goals, notes, cutout pictures from magazines and photos, and essentially everything you dream and that you are intending on manifesting will go inside this box. Dream big!! Every time you put something inside, you will say, "It is." I love to look inside my box at the collections of pictures, notes that I wrote to myself, and goals that I have set for myself. It is really amazing how pretty much everything that I put inside my box has already manifested or is in the process of manifesting. So every time I put something new inside my box I get really excited because I know it's on its way. It's kind of like a really special vision board or another fun Law of Attraction tool. Give it a try. It's really fun!

Tap into Your Spirituality

Whatever you have as a spiritual practice or religion, or if you don't have any, this is a good time to get curious or really dive into it. Go deeper into meditation, yoga, and reading books about them so that you can reach your highest self. Because you are so much more open-minded now and in a place of empathy and compassion, you will take this in so much more easily and absorb all of the qualities and teachings that they offer. Once I started to open myself to new experiences and really dive into my spirituality, I found that I have been able to uncover so many more layers of myself and have such a deep love for myself and reverence for the world that I have never experienced before.

The first self-help book I read, *The Seat of the Soul* by Gary Zukav, blew me away and left me completely hooked on wanting to learn more. I was really blessed to have an amazing friend who always pointed me in the right direction and downloaded books and shared his spiritual and meditation practices with me, but nowadays, all you have to do is go online or find meetups to gather this information if you need it. There is so much opportunity for spiritual enrichment now because there is so much access to so many amazing books and so much wonderful information online. Take advantage of it and start practicing.

Travel Somewhere New

If it's possible, book that trip to Paris you have always dreamed about or check out that new state park or those trails in your state. Even if it's just to another state or another park, traveling to a new place can be like an amazing and brief start over for your brain. Imagine stepping off an airplane into new surroundings, new cultures, new foods, new music, and new customs. This is exciting on its own, but traveling to a new place also helps broaden your perspective, open your mind, and get you a real-life education perfect for your new life chapter. It is something you can keep forever in your memories.

If you can't leave the country just yet, you can still create a lifetime of memories and amazing experiences by visiting new places within your reach. Get out there and visit a new park, a new beach, or another state. The point is to go somewhere new once a year, if possible.

↻ LET'S RECAP _____

- Practice and use Visualization as a powerful tool to align your emotions and thoughts to your future
  - Do a self-inventory check to get clear about your wants and don't wants

- Look into altruism as a healthy break from pain that will help others and release stress to you.
  - Get curious about your spirituality
- Travel somewhere new and make lifetime memories

Chapter 9:

Become Inspired and Inspire Others

Healing Crystals: Beryl, Rose Quartz, Citrine

By now you are feeling quite different about things. You know that divorce can be a deep, bottomless, exhausting well if you choose the wrong path, so I commend you on choosing to go through it compassionately and carefully. You also know what an amazing, unique, and powerful being you are. You understand that you will still have ups and downs, but now you can see that you are going to be okay. You have realized that you have been given this amazing gift of a new life and that soon enough your pain will be history. You also now know that your ex was here for a reason and that all your past relationships offer you an opportunity to learn something about yourself. You now have a great, valuable life lesson and powerful tools under your belt, and you are learning to become who you were truly meant to be—your best and most authentic self. And that feels freaking fantastic!

When you feel aligned with whom you are meant to be, there is a new undeniable energy about you, and you can't help but feel inspired to pass it on. You feel the need to help others through their journey. You feel this sense of having traveled through a war and making it to the other side so that you can live to tell about it.

What Is Your Calling?

When I went through my divorce, I knew I wanted to help others with their struggle. I reached out to my friends and anyone I knew who was going through a similar situation and offered myself to help. I understood at that moment that these individuals were entering a monumental time in their lives that could go two ways: they could either use this opportunity to discover what the lesson was that this situation was offering and become empowered by this knowledge, or they could spiral into self-destructive behavior. So I absolutely had to help. And the pain that I had gone through was so unbearable that I wanted to see if I might be able provide some relief to others. If I could somehow show them through my experience that they were going to be fine, then it would be another great benefit of my journey. Why not pay it forward?

When you help others, you not only help change their lives but you also inspire generosity and compassion in others. It's like you are contributing to the good in the world. In addition, being in this space of helping and inspiring introduces you to many like-minded people, some of whom end up becoming a pivotal part of your life. Instead of being disconnected from the world, you become fully aware and part of it in a different way—in a compassionate way. You also model this behavior for your children and pass on this goodness to them; because, as you know, parents are the biggest role models to their children and this will truly help shape their lives in such a positive way.

Watching your children make compassionate gestures keeps you inspired. Paying it forward erases ego. Because you have gone through a life-altering experience, you no longer take many things for granted. You have a completely different perspective of whatever you thought you knew about pain, divorce, and breakups, and you honor and respect those going through it.

"Be the change you want to see in the world."
— Gandhi

Chapter 10:

Obstacles

Healing Crystals: Black Tourmaline, Peridot, Hematite

Healing Is Not Linear

The reason I need you to understand this is because many people view healing as A, the place where you are, to B, the place you end up—*healed*. The reality is that there can be A, G, Z, or B. What I mean is that you can get on the path to healing and still fall off the path. For instance, you might get an unexpected call from your ex or run into him, and you might find yourself overcome with a flood of emotions. You may even feel a little like you did in the beginning. You might want to ditch this whole process and run back under your covers. But this is when it's crucial to remember all of the hard work you have put in and all of the knowledge you have acquired about yourself and the lessons you have learned. No matter what, you can't unlearn this. It is in you.

It's perfectly normal to feel emotional running into your ex, but if you take a pause and really observe, you will see the difference in how you are processing these emotions now. Really not quite the same, right? You have fought too hard in this war.

There are also several obstacles that might try to throw you off course.

You have opened up and peeked inside, and now you realize this is what you have been avoiding all of these years. Getting to know the real you? Eeeeeeeeekkkkkkk! Dealing with your past might seem too much for you. Equip yourself and be ready to fight off the gremlins!

You might realize that in order to move forward and heal from your core, changes have to happen. And many people have resistance to change.

You might want to go back to the old familiar place or leave the door open because, maybe, by some miracle, your ex might call and want to reconcile with you.

You might tell yourself that you feel too depressed or confused to commit to anything or try something new.

You might feel like this takes too much work, time, and effort. (By the way, if you feel like you are genuinely depressed and are a danger to yourself or others, please seek psychiatric help immediately.)

You might find yourself immersed in challenges at work, and these things might zap your attention from beginning this work. Your inner critics (those darn gremlins) will arrive and try to keep you from healing and try to pull you back into misery (the known). Any of these obstacles may arrive. It is important that you are aware. It is mostly important that you prepare and remind yourself that all of them are mechanisms to pull you back and keep you from changing. Your mind doesn't like change. And your ego wants control, and sometimes that means staying in the past.

You bought this book for a reason, and you are not going to be swayed back. You have come too far in your journey. You are ready to move forward and keep going. However, if you are still feeling a little tender, like you might go back, and you could use a little extra support, this is the time to consider hiring a life coach or a therapist to help you stay on target and reach your goal. They will also help you to hold yourself accountable and listen without any judgment or outside interference.

I Would Be Honored to Work with You

Hiring me as your coach for the process

You now understand that time does not heal everything, and you need to put in some work. By working with me, we can start right at the beginning, right where you are, and really dive into the program. You will start to see and feel results much faster than doing it alone because even though I am not here to make you do anything, I will be your accountability partner.

There is a certain power in stating a commitment to a life coach on a weekly basis. You will learn how to keep those gremlins and self-limiting beliefs from interfering with your goals. I will be there to offer insights when you feel stuck. There is no judgment. This is your journey. By making commitments, even really tiny ones, you will be moving forward on your healing scale. And having a life coach by your side will help you stay clear, focused, and committed to your healing process. I will help you see your full potential where you will be inspired and motivated to keep stretching and growing, and I will champion and celebrate each of your successes and milestones, no matter how big or small, to keep you excited and motivated. I will hold your focus and keep your vision alive when you feel like you might start to fall off track. I will help you see beyond where you are right now and think *big*, because that's what you deserve.

Chapter 11:

Conclusion

Healing Crystals: Rose Quartz, Rhodocrosite, Morganite

"Life Is a Journey, from Phase to Phase."

You can now see how you can turn this broken heart into the best thing that ever happened to you. It just takes willingness on your part and an open mind. My first self-help book changed everything for me. If you allow it, this book can change everything for you, too.

Working through the grief of my divorce changed my entire life. I was free. I was open. For the first time in my life, I was authentic, and I loved myself. When I look back at my life while I was in my previous marriage, I see a shallow, empty woman who didn't really think much about herself other than what she was wearing or how good her hair and makeup looked. There was no looking inward. It was about how good things looked from the outside and to the outside world.

I find scribbles from the initial period of my separation from my ex-husband that make me gasp. It's astonishing, even to myself, to see how good I was at hiding, and how great I was at telling others that I was okay and that I was so tough. But everything was a lie. The truth was that I was in agony. I was far from okay. Despite the smile I threw on my face or the sexy clothes clinging to my body on the dance floor, while I was trying to run away, I felt empty and broken inside. I had been cast out from my comfortable reality, and I was terrified. I felt like the wind could blow the wrong way, and I would fall to pieces.

These days, looking at my journals, oh boy are things quite different. The journals are filled with uplifting passages and steps. They are filled with quotes, poetry, gratefulness messages, music, intentions, goals, and affirmations. These entries reflect a much different person, an empowered and inspired woman who is excited about life and who will never ever stop getting up, going forward, and diving inward to continue with this beautiful transformation and growth. I have remarried, ironically enough to another man named Eric. My husband and I celebrated our six-year wedding anniversary this year. We have a beautiful, spirited five-year-old little boy together.

We live in a beautiful home with my stepdaughter and our two cats. It's amazing to look back at eleven years ago, when I was in such agony in the midst of my horrible divorce, thinking that I would never love again.

It's amazing to compare these periods of my life. Everything back then was so shallow, empty, and false. Now, it's so much about reflecting, forgiving, mindfulness and compassion. I now live to help others with self-love, healing, and strength. If I were to be an outsider looking in, it would be evident that this was clearly the evolution of someone who had suffered and had spent years of peeling back layers to find herself. Although some of these times have not been easy, it has always been an interesting and humbling journey. It has been rewarding to say the least. The way my life has changed and unfolded after this intense period of suffering, not just from my divorce but from my little brother's death, is still unbelievable to me. Nothing manifested in the way I imagined. It has been so much better! Through my gratefulness and appreciation, I find myself always eager to reach out to others and assist them in crossing over to their own healing path and their own self-discovery. There is nothing more inspiring than being a part of or witnessing their journey and their destination. The death of my marriage, although traumatic, has been the best thing that ever happened to me. It changed my life forever and in the best way possible. Once I decided to go on this healing, self-discovery path, I stopped existing, and I started living.

LET'S RECAP _____

First and foremost, you are going to be okay! Your heartbreak offers you a chance to unlock the troubles from the past, and all the pain that you have kept bottled up. You now have an opportunity to work and heal them. You now have tools to help you release negative emotions, ground and center yourself, and reprogram old habits into positive ones.

You understand the importance of setting intentions and affirmations and how they serve as a roadmap. You accept the ending of your relationship as something that had to happen in order for you to grow and be the best version of yourself, and you don't look at it with regret. You learned about forgiving yourself and your ex-partner, and releasing the pain and judgment. You also learned about forgiveness being a process, so you can take it nice and slow. It's okay if you are not there yet.

You've done amazing work since your breakup, and you see this time as an invaluable place to reinvent and love yourself in a whole new way, and you understand the importance of being happy alone before you can be happy in a new relationship. You know that there are many obstacles that might try to pull you back and keep you from growing and changing the paradigm. Lastly, you know what a warrior you are, how far you have come, how deep your dive has been, and how it is your choice to keep moving forward and reaching for the stars in your amazing life.

I hope this book helps guide you into your healing path and that it helps you uncover a new, healthy, and beautiful you. My wish is that you will find yourself to be full of hope, peace and acceptance. I hope you feel clear and emotionally grounded. That you are able to break the emotional attachment you have to your ex, and that you move forward and make empowered choices that align you to your higher self. You are a beautiful, powerful and worthy human being. Do not sell yourself short or settle for anything other than the best.

In the book *The Heart of the Soul*, Gary Zukav teaches that we are all students in the School of Life. If you can adapt this philosophy and keep this message in the back of your mind, you will not have regrets, you will instead look at all obstacles and inner experiences as opportunities for growth and healing, and in each instance, you will move forward with new lessons learned, new knowledge, new tools, and a better outlook on life that you will pass on to others. I know you are doing wonderful work and are rocking it, but if you need additional support, I would be honored to help you on your journey. If you want to speak with me one-on-one to see if we can work together, please visit my website www.myselftruly.com or email me at carmen@myselftruly.com.

Acknowledgments

I have been so blessed with an amazing support system in life and with writing this book and would like to thank all of them. First, I will begin with my husband, Eric Silvestro; this book would have not been possible without his amazing patience and support. Thank you for always loving and believing in me. I love you.

My amazing parents, Miguel and Julia Ortiz, for teaching me about strength and compassion, for demonstrating so much resilience in the face of much adversity, for loving me unconditionally, and for always being so proud and supportive of me, thank you.

Thanks to my siblings: Miguel, Patty, John, Luis, Jacqueline, Michelle, and of course my little brother, Omar, who lives on in all of us, always.

My team of Angels: my sisters Patty and Jackie and my dearest friend, Carolynn Saraco, you all supported me through my darkest times, watched me fall and stand up many times, and cheered my perseverance and triumphs as if your own. Thank you from the bottom of my heart.

Many thanks also go to the following people: My friend and ex-boss, Hugh Schwartzberg, for his many kind words of encouragement. All my friends and soul sisters from the QSCA, especially Geraldine Logan and Tammy Hall.

Thanks to my mentors, teachers, and inspirations: Anthony Licata, Gail Belluardo, Tamara Tosun, Amy Sherwood, Lisandra Jimenez, Angela Lauria. My editor Nkechi Obi for keeping me sane throughout this process. All the angels from The Author Incubator. Thank you to David Hancock and the Morgan James Publishing team for helping me bring this book to print. And finally to all my private coaching clients, especially Jolina Nevolo and Jacqueline Ortiz, who touch my life and inspire me to do more every day.

Thank You

Thank you, to you, my reader. I am inspired by your courage and willingness to take the first step toward your healing path. I hold the highest vision for you, and I would be honored to be able to continue to support you on your journey.

Because of my own divorce struggles, I have become really passionate about helping people who are suffering through a painful breakup, divorce, or are trying to find love again. When my marriage ended eleven years ago, I felt utterly destroyed and alone. It was the hardest experience of my life. When I discovered a way to heal and was able to open my heart again, I felt unbelievably free and empowered, and I vowed to help as many people as I could get through this painful phase and into the lives they deserve.

I would love to learn more about your healing journey. Please send me a note on Facebook or Instagram, and for more information or to take a free half hour class, visit my website www.Myselftruly.com.

Thank you again!

About the Author

Carmen Silvestro is a certified life coach. Her passion is helping people take back control in their lives after heartbreak from a breakup or divorce. While preparing to return to a twenty-year career as an accounting and human resource manager that she took a break from to raise her child, she realized that her calling is making a difference in people's lives. She also realized that for many people to truly overcome the pain from divorce or breakup, they need more than just conventional therapy.

Carmen became certified as a life coach through the *Quantum Success Coaching Academy*. She combines her experience of getting through her own painful divorce and achieving monumental life changes with the research and information learned through coaching clients to develop programs for her one-on-one clients and group coaching.

She looks back at her divorce and each life challenging experience with such gratitude for what it has taught her, and she sees how it has shaped her and gotten her to where she is today. She believes that every human being has a fire inside of them, that once ignited makes them unstoppable.

Carmen lives in Whippany, New Jersey with her husband, their rambunctious five-year-old boy, stepdaughter, and two cats. She loves music, art, poetry, meditating, hiking, inspirational books and challenging workouts.

To learn more about the author visit:

Websites:

www.myselftruly.com, www.carmensilvestro.com

Facebook:

https://www.facebook.com/carmenshannon

You can also email her for one-on-one or group coaching: carmen@myselftruly.com

CPSIA information can be obtained
at www.ICGtesting.com
Printed in the USA
JSHW041556120421
13501JS00001B/114